Tom Leonard

THE ARAB CREATION MYTH

THE ARAB CREATION MYTH

Abdullah al-Udhari

Archangel

B V

PRAGUE

First published 1997 in Prague
by A r c h a n g e l
in association with BV Nakladatelství
Revoluční 28, 110 00 Prague 1,
Czech Republic

Designed by Miloš Novák
Printed by UNI GRAFIA, a. s.

ISBN 80 901800 5 1

For Laura

Laura womangarden centres the green

These are the myths of the ancient.
Qur'an: al-Mu'minum: 83

CONTENTS

INTRODUCTION

The Continuity of the Arab Tradition

When I lost my first milk tooth my mother told me: "Dont worry my son. Dont throw your tooth away, but keep it in your pocket until dawn. And before sunrise get up and go to the hill overlooking the wadi and wait for the morning sun. And when you see the sun rising behind the mountains take your tooth out of your pocket and hold it between your thumb and forefinger, then face the sun and throw the tooth in the eye of the sun and say: 'O sun, replace this tooth with a better one that has a sunlight glow. Take this donkey tooth and give me the tooth of a gazelle.' And the sun will replace your milk tooth with the strong and sparkling tooth of a gazelle. And when you lose your other milk teeth do the same thing with each of them."

As the years rolled on I began to read Jahili (pre Islam) poetry and to my surprise I discovered that the Jahili poets invariably allude to the milk tooth ritual like the one I performed as a little boy.

I was also surprised to discover that the milk tooth ritual was performed by children throughout the Arab World. This discovery made me explore the immensely rich Arab folk tradition and try to relate it to the Jahili mythology preserved in the Qur'an and the Hadith (the dictums of the Prophet Muhammad), and in classical Arab literature.

My research into the folk tradition and the mythology of Jahiliyya led me to believe that if the milk tooth ritual has remained a living tradition inspite of sixteen centuries of Islam strictures, then there is no reason why the Jahili myths could not have survived from the time of the Nuh (Noah) Flood to the time when they were collected and edited in the Islam (622-661 CE), Umayyad (661-750) and Abbasid (750-1258) periods, or to the present time.

The stories that make up *The Arab Creation Myth* were a living tradition in my home town when I was a little boy. During the month of Ramadan, a storyteller used to come to our street and sit infront of our house overlooked by Mount Aroos and Mount Sabir. The children of the neighbourhood and myself would gather around the storyteller and in silent reverence listen to him recounting the tales of the folk heroes, believing every word he said. Among the tales he told were those of Iblees and the Shayaateen, Adam and Hawwa, and Haabeel and Qaabeel. Sometimes he retold the stories of paradise and hell, heaven and earth, and what we learnt from him was that Iblees was the greatest and most loveable hero who had absolute power over the earth, and all the rulers of the world ruled on his behalf.

The storyteller used to tell us that precious stones possessed magical qualities which could realise whatever one desired. And Yemen was once a land littered with precious stones, and dotted with gold and silver mountains and hills of musk. And the ancient Arabs of Yemen built their homes with precious stones, silver and gold and alabaster. And they grew all kinds of sweetscented trees with unimaginably beautiful flowers and deliciously fleshy fruits. And when it rained the land was a breath of freshly scented air. And Yemen was so fabulously rich that all her people were incredibly wealthy merchants who held regular trade fairs to trade with one another, and whatever they did not need they exported to other lands.

The storyteller would go on describing paradise, especially its fruit bearing gemtrees, its singing and talking jewel birds, its palaces and houses and tents, which were made of precious stones, silver and gold. And he always cited the story of the mythical king Shaddad b. 'Ad, who set out to create a paradisial city on earth called *Iram dhat al-'Imad* (Iram the City of Pillars), which had fruit bearing gemtrees and palaces made of precious stones and silver and gold, to rival Allah's paradise, and how Allah punished him by making Iram the City of Pillars disappear just as he was about to ride into it with his army and entourage, who were then destroyed by a fiery storm. And the storyteller assured us that Iram the City of Pillars reappears every thousand years, and the last time it reappeared it was seen by a man in the reign of the Caliph 'Umar (584-644).

The storyteller also used to say that Mount Aroos resembled one of the mountains in heaven, and that Aden was an earthly copy of Jannat Adan (third paradise) and could be seen from Mount Aroos on a fine and clear day. And since those days my dream has been to climb Mount Aroos so as to have a glimpse of Aden, the earthly paradise.

My mother also used to tell me stories about paradise and heaven and hell, Adam and Hawwa, Iblees and the Shayaateen, and angels serving Allah, protecting people and battling with Iblees and the Shayaateen.

I started learning the Qur'an at the age of four and I finished reading it by the age of seven. I was spellbound by the sound of the Qur'an words and the stories they told. The stories that appealed to me most were those of the ancient Arabs and the stories of creation, especially those connected with Adam and Hawwa, and Iblees and the angels. Sometimes I would pester my mother to tell me more about these stories, particularly the bits I could not grasp.

The Qur'an stories kept haunting me until I went to university and began to study the Qur'an, the Hadith and Jahili literature. While studying Jahili literature I discovered I was exploring a familiar world and reliving my childhood, because the world in which I grew up retained most of the terms of reference and nuances of Jahiliyya.

In the early sixties I read the Gilgamesh epic and I was struck by a passage describing trees of precious stones bearing fruits of gems, which reminded me of the paradisial gardens and Iram the City of Pillars of king Shaddad, and of the similar magical gardens of the caliphs of Baghdad. It seems the gardens of fruit bearing gemtrees and talking jewel birds and animals draw on a tradition as old as the history of man in the Arab World.

I then read the creation myths of the Sumerians, Babylonians, Egyptians and Ugarits, and of cultures not related to the Arab World. After I read all the creation myths I could lay my hands on, I began to wonder why was there no epic that told the creation myth of the Arabs, inspite of the fact that there were stories of the creation of the world in the Qur'an, the Hadith, classical literature and folk tradition, as well as poems and songs attributed to Adam, Iblees and the Houris, and dialogues between Allah and Jibreel, Allah and Iblees, Allah and Adam, Adam and Hawwa and Adam and Iblees.

I remember when I first came across the poems of Adam and Iblees, the songs of the Houris and the dialogues, I was so excited by my discovery that I started looking for the epic from which these fragments I thought were culled. While I was searching for the epic of the Arab Genesis myth I stumbled on the titles of four Jahili lost works: *Kitab Allah* (The Book of Allah), *Kitab al-Bad'* (The Book of Genesis), also known as *Kitab al-Mubtada* (The Book of Genesis), *Bad'al-Khalq* (The Genesis of Creation) and *Al-Tawrat* (The Torah). And what I found interesting about the title of the fourth work was that whenever the Arab mythologists Ka'b al-Ahbar (548-642), Abdullah b. Salam (d. 663) and Wahb b. Munabbih (654-732) talked about the Ka'ba and other Arab terms of reference not mentioned in the Hebrew Torah, they said they got their information from *Al-Tawrat* (The Torah). As 'Tawrat' (sing. Tawra) is an Arabiyya and Hebrew word (Ar. light, message sent to the people; Heb. Teachings), and as Ka'b al-Ahbar and Abdullah b. Salam were highly learned rabbis before their conversion to Islam, and Wahb b. Munabbih was familiar with the Hebrew Torah, the three mythologists would not have alluded to *Al-Tawrat* when talking, for example, about the Ka'ba or the Tooba Tree if their terms of reference had not been the Arab Torah. So I looked for the Jahili lost works but to no avail.

I then began to examine the Umayyad and Abbasid texts dealing with Jahiliyya. To my surprise I found that the style and language of these texts have more in common with Jahili writing than with the writing of the period to which they were ascribed. The texts also bear no relation to the style of writing of their supposed authors.

Some Umayyad and Abbasid writers edited Jahili prose texts and published them as their own works. A close reading of these texts shows that their style and language differ from those of their editors. For example, the style and language of *Kitab al-Tijan* (The Book of Crowns), attributed to Wahb b. Munabbih, are different from the style and language of his other works in general and of the works of Umayyad and Abbasid writers in particular. Also some of the themes as well as the style and language of *Kitab al-Tijan* overlap with the style and language and some of the themes of *Akhbar al-Yaman* (The History of Yemen) by the Jahili historian and raconteur Ubaid b. Shariyya (d. 686) who was about a hundred years old when he recounted the history of Yemen to the Umayyad Caliph

Mu'awiya (603-680). Further, the same accounts in both books are quoted in a similar style and language by Umayyad and Abbasid historians but attributed to writers other than Wahb and Ubaid.

One of the works attributed to Wahb b. Munabbih is *Kitab al-Mubtada* (The Book of Genesis). Although this book has not yet been discovered fragments of it survive in quotation form. Arab mythologists, historians and Qur'an commentators invariably refer to this book and to works by other writers of creation myths. If we compare the style and language of Wahb's Book of Genesis with the style and language of the creation myths of other writers, we will find them remarkably similar, which means that the creation myths come from the same source. Moreover, the style and language of all these creation myths betray a Jahili origin.

Inspite of two hundred years of Jahili scholarship, our knowledge of Jahiliyya is less than skin deep. Why should this be the case when there is ample material from the Jahiliyya? The reason for this superficial scholarship is that the Arabists tend to dismiss the Jahili texts as unauthentic without vetting them to determine their authenticity. They also disregard the Islam, Umayyad and Abbasid accounts of Jahiliyya as unreliable unless they are corroborated by non-Arab sources.

The Arabists are under the illusion that they have a better grasp of Arabiyya and Arab culture than the classical Arab scholars. This knowing-it-all attitude has made life easier for the Arabists and given them scope to roam around freely in theory land. The problem with this perception is that its proponents, who have a limited knowledge of Arabiyya and are thus incapable of reading the classical texts let alone distinguishing the style of individual authors and of different periods have already made up their mind what the Jahili world ought to have been rather than what it actually was. They picture the Jahiliyya as a world inhabited by illiterate nomads and semiliterate sedentary people living on the fringes of the Arabian Peninsula, who had no concept of bookwriting, and their way of life aped that of their civilised neighbours.

In the light of new works being edited in recent years, and the reediting of published classics, it is time to brush aside the dated and blinkered views on Jahiliyya and the subsequent periods, and reassess Arab culture in general and Jahili culture in particular. It is also imperative to take into account how the classical Arabs perceived their ancient and contemporary world; by so doing we will be able to fully appreciate and understand their achievements.

One of the areas that has been neglected by the Arabists is Arab mythology. Most of the Arabists presume that the Jahilis never had a mythology of their own and the few myths they had were borrowed from their neighbours. Their presumption is not founded on a thorough investigation of Jahili mythology but on minor overlapping details.

On the other hand, *The Arab Creation Myth*, which is a reconstruction of the Arab Genesis based on over thirty years of research, proves that despite the minor overlappings with the Sumerian, Babylonian, Ugaritic, Egyptian and Hebrew myths of creation due to their common origin, the Jahili creation myth is distinct and far more developed than all the other creation myths.

II

The Jahiliyya

The period covering the history of the Arabs from the earliest times to the rise of Islam is called the Jahiliyya. The precise meaning of the term is unclear. The traditional definition of Jahiliyya as "the age of spiritual darkness" reflects a religious bias based on the unqualified interpretation of certain Qur'an *ayas* (verses) in which the Jahilis were taken to task for seeing Allah in terms of intermediaries. This unfavourable view, which gained currency after the establishment of Islam, has over the centuries blurred our appreciation and understanding of the immensely rich and varied Jahili civilisations out of which Islam was born. The Qur'an, the Hadith and Jahili literature show that the Jahiliyya was far from being a spiritual and cultural desert. On the contrary, it was a spiritually and culturally fertile period whose achievements shaped and determined the course of Islam, and left an indelible mark on the imagination of the peoples who came under the influence of Islam.

As there is no historical justification for the current meaning of Jahiliyya as "the age of spiritual darkness", it is possible that the intended subtle nuances of the term had either been lost by the time it became necessary to define it, or they were deliberately overlooked because they clashed with the established view that enhanced Islam. A likely explanation of Jahiliyya is that, since the Jahilis were divided along triboregional lines, they failed to project a vision capable of creating a political, cohesive force that could have channelled their resources towards a clearly defined goal similar to that of

Islam. Another likely explanation is that the term Jahiliyya could simply mean "the preceding period" or "the past", or as the grammarian Ibn Khalawaih (d. 980) describes it, "the period before Islam". This interpretation is endorsed by the Qur'an, the Hadith, the Prophet's sermons, the remarks of the Caliph 'Umar (584-644), the Sahabis (the Prophet's companions) and by the Jahili poet 'Amr b. Ma'di Karib (d. 642). According to one tradition the term Jahiliyya was first used by a woman who asked the Prophet about some camels she obtained in "Jahiliyya".

The theologian Zamakhshari (1067-1144) says the term Jahiliyya evokes two different ways of life encompassing the Jahili and the Islam eras. Jahiliyya in the Jahili sense denotes an intercessionary and sybaritic way of life; and in the Islam sense it denotes only a sybaritic way of life. On the other hand, the term was probably coined to convey an ambivalent attitude resulting from an insufficient and confused knowledge of the period in question.

The early history of most civilisations is in the main preserved in the oral tradition written many centuries after the events described had occurred. This is true of the Sumerians, Babylonians, Greeks, Romans and Arabs. Just as the epics of the Sumerians, Babylonians, Greeks and Romans embody the memory of their respective early history, Jahili poetry, Jahili *hadiths* (histories), Jahili *akhbar* (historical narratives), Jahili *siras* (epics), Jahili *amthal* (proverbs, parables and fables), Ayyam al-'Arab (The Heroic Days of the Arabs), the Qur'an, the Hadith, *Akhbar al-Yaman* (The History of Yemen) and *Kitab al-Tijan* (The Book of Crowns), have kept the memory of the Arabs alive for posterity. While the languages and the oral tradition of the above peoples died with the demise of the people concerned, the Arab language and oral tradition have continued to thrive up to the present day. The milk tooth ritual and the language in which it is couched are a living proof of the continuity of the Arab tradition.

One tradition regards the Nuh Flood as a turning point in the history of Jahiliyya. The period before the Flood is called *Ma Qabl al-Tawfan* (Before the Flood) and *al-Jahiliyya al-Ula* (The First Jahiliyya), and runs from the landing of Adam and Hawwa on earth to the Nuh Flood. The period from the Flood to the rise of Islam is called Jahiliyya. Another tradition sees the Nuh Flood as the starting point of Jahiliyya, and considers the period from the landing of Adam and Hawwa on earth to the Nuh Flood as *Ma Qabl al-Jahiliyya* (Before Jahiliyya or Pre History).

The Jahili oath *Bidhat al-Wad'* (By Noah's Ark) and the annual fasting and celebration of the 'Ashura Day (10th Muharram) on which the Jahilis commemorated the day Nuh came out of the Ark with his eighty companions, as well as the Flood myths, like the story of Nuh rewarding the dove with a green necklace for its success in finding dry land, affirm the Flood experience of the Jahilis, and lend credibility to the Arabs' belief in regarding the Flood as the starting point of their history. The Jahili proverb *Ma huwa illa Ghurab Nuh* (He is like Noah's Raven), which describes a man who goes away and never returns, and the tradition that the city of Azaal (modern day Sanaa, the capital of Yemen) and its twentystorey Palace of Ghumdan were built by Sam (Shem) b. Nuh are further illustrations of the Jahilis' link with the Flood.

Tradition divides the Jahiliyya into five periods, and dates each period by choosing an epochmaking event centred around pivotal figures as the starting point of each period:

1. *Jahiliyyat al-'Arab al-Ba'ida* (The Jahiliyya of the Extinct Arabs or The Jahiliyya of the Lost Arab Civilisations),

4000 BCE - 1700 BCE, starts with Nuh coming out of the Ark with his eighty companions and founding the town of Thamanin (eighty).

2. *Al-Jahiliyya al-Jahla'* (The Distant Jahiliyya), 1700 BCE - 700 BCE, starts with the rebuilding of the Ka'ba by Ibrahim (Abraham) and his son Isma'il (Ishmael).
3. *Al-Jahiliyya al-Qadima* (The Ancient Jahiliyya), 700 BCE - 100 CE, starts with the return of the patriarch Ma'add to Mecca after the death of his father 'Adnan in the Nebuchednezzar's wars.
4. *Al-Jahiliyya al-Wusta* (The Middle Jahiliyya), 100 CE - 400 CE, starts with the establishment of the Azd kingdom in Oman and Iraq by the poet Malik b. Fahm al-Azdi.
5. *Al-Jahiliyya al-Muta'akhkhira* (The Late Jahiliyya), 400 CE - 622 CE, starts with Qusayy b. Kilab assuming the custodianship of the Ka'ba and ends with the advent of Islam. Qusayy was the great-great-great-grand-father of the Prophet Muhammad.

III

The Arabs

The Arab tradition breaks up the Arabs into two groups. The first group is called *al-'Arab al-'Ariba* (The Pure Arabs) and *'Arab al-Musnad* (The Original Arabs), which includes the 'Adites, the Thamudis, the 'Amalikites, the First Jurhumis, the 'Abd Dakhmis, the Umaimis, the 'Abilis, the Jasimis, the Tasmis, the Jadisis and the descendants of Ya'rub b. Qahtan, the grandson of the 'Adite prophet Hud b. 'Abir (Eber) and the ancestor of Bilqis the queen of Sheba, who moved out of Iraq soon after the Winds of Babil (Tower of Babel) incident and settled in Yemen. The second group is called *al-'Arab al-Musta'riba* (The Arabised Arabs), who are the descendants of the prophet Isma'il (Ishmael).

The urban, *badiya* (country) and *bedu* Arabs are called *'Arab*. The Arabs of the *badiya* are called *A'rab* and the nomadic Arabs are called *bedu*. The *badiya* and *bedu* Arabs who settle in towns are called *Nabàt* (urban) and *Hadar* (urban), and the urban Arabs who move to the *badiya* or become nomadic are called *'Arab*.

It is unclear how the Arabs acquired their name. One Jahili tradition relates that the Arabs were named after Ya'rub b. Qahtan. Another tradition intimates that the Arabs were named after their homeland 'Araba (known also by its plural form 'Arabat), which is the ancient name of the Arabian Peninsula. A third tradition says the Arabs were named after the Tihama town 'Araba where Isma'il's children grew up. A fourth tradition holds that the Arabs were named after their Arabiyya

(Arab language) which the angel Jibreel (Gabriel) taught them to speak.

In the Hebrew tradition Eber is the father of Peleg and Joktan, and Peleg is the ancestor of Abraham. In the Arab tradition ʻAbir (Eber) is the father of al-Qasim (Peleg) and Hud who is the father of Qahtan (Joktan), the ancestor of the Arabs. Since the Arabs and the Hebrews trace their descent to ʻAbir (Eber), then it is possible that the ethnic terms *ʻArab* and *Aʻrab*, like the ethnic term *ʻIbri* (Hebrew), are derived from *ʻAbir* but in a metathesised form. The meaning of *ʻAbir* and Eber in Arabiyya and Hebrew is "one who crosses over", which suggests that once upon a time, long before Ibrahim, the Arabs and the Hebrews were one people who, at a certain point in history, broke up and went their separate ways. And this explains why there are strong affinities between Arabiyya and Hebrew. Furthermore, the name of Jacob's son Yahuda (Judah) is reminiscent of the name of the ʻAdite monotheist prophet Hud who does not appear in the Hebrew Genesis nor do the ʻAdites for that matter. The prophet Hud is buried in the Ahqaf land of the ʻAdites in Yemen, and his tomb has been a centre of pilgrimage since Jahiliyya.

The Arab tradition has it that Ibrahim's son Ismaʻil grew up among the Jurhumi Arabs of Mecca, who were the descendants of Jurhum b. Qahtan according to one account, and the descendants of Jurhum, the son of an ʻAmalikite woman and an expelled angel who landed in Mecca, according to another account. Ismaʻil adopted the Arabiyya of the Jurhumis and married Raʻla, the daughter of the Jurhumi king Mudad b. ʻAmr al-Jurhumi, and had twelve sons. One of the major patriarchs of the Arabs is ʻAdnan b. Udad who traces his descent to Ismaʻil's son Qaidar. When Nebuchednezzar's armies swept across North Arabia and wiped out ʻAdnan and his Arab forces, an angel saved and looked after ʿAdnan's twelve-year-old son Maʿadd. After the war the angel took Maʿadd back to Mecca where he settled down and had many children. The most famous of Maʿadd's children was Nizar whose four sons Iyad, Rabiʿa, Mudar and Anmar became the patriarchs of the major Arab tribes like Shaiban, Tamim, ʿAbs, Taghlib, Bakr, Asad and Quraish, that dominated the political scene of the Late Jahiliyya. The patriarch Mudar is the ancestor of the Prophet Muhammad.

IV

The Arabiyya

The Arab tradition relates that the Jahilis spoke one common language, with minor triboregional idiosyncracies. The same tradition traces this common language back to the time of Isma'il b. Ibrahim, and makes a distinction between the language spoken by the Arabs before Isma'il and the language spoken since Isma'il. The pre Isma'il language is called *al-'Arabiyya al-Ula* (The First Arabiyya or Ancient Arabiyya) and *Musnad* (The Original Arabiyya) that emphasises the archaicness of the Arabiyya which, according to one tradition, the angel Jibreel taught the 'Adites, the Thamudis, the 'Amalikites, the First Jurhumis, the 'Abd Dakhmis, the Umaimis, the 'Abilis, the Jasimis, the Tasmis, the Jadisis and the Qahtanis to speak during the Winds of Babil incident.

The story goes that when the town of Thamanin became too small for its growing population, some of its inhabitants moved out and founded a new city within an area of sixty square kilometres and called it Babil (Babylon). By the time of the Babili king Nimrud the Great, a contemporary of al-Qasim (Peleg), the population of Babil had grown to one hundred thousand people who spoke one language and were dominated by seventy two families. As the Flood memory was still haunting the Babilis, the seventy two families decided to build the Mijdal (Castle), which was two thousand and five hundred metres high and one thousand and five hundred metres wide, to protect them from floods and diseases. Allah was not pleased with the Mijdal which He regarded as a challenge to His Will. Allah ordered Jibreel, the angel of war and winds and earthquakes, to babble up the speech of the seventy two families so they might not understand one another, and to release the South Wind, the North Wind, the East Wind and the West Wind to destroy the Mijdal. Jibreel babbled up the speech of the seventy two families and taught each family to speak a different language, then released the Four Winds that blew each family along a separate road. Jibreel destroyed the Mijdal with one of his wings, and the Four Winds scattered about the falling masonry. One of the languages Jibreel taught the seventy two families was Musnad Arabiyya.

The Musnad speakers found their way to Yemen where they settled and became known as the *'Arab al-Musnad* (The Original Arabs) and *al-'Arab al-'Ariba* (The Pure Arabs). By the Late Jahiliyya the Qahtanis were the only survivors of the Musnad Arabs. And since then the term Musnad has been used to refer solely to the Jahili Qahtanis, their language and their script. Some classical Arab traditionists went so far as to say that Adam's son Hibatullah (Seth) spoke a form of Musnad Arabiyya. Could the Musnad Arabiyya of Hibatullah be the proto Arabiyya out of which all the Arabiyya related languages evolved? Hopefully, future excavations in the Arabian Peninsula will throw light on this question.

According to another tradition, when Nuh came out of the Ark with his eighty companions they went down a wadi and founded the town of Thamanin. One night, while Nuh's eighty companions were asleep, Jibreel appeared to them in a dream and taught them to speak eighty different languages, one of which was the Arabiyya. When they woke they were babbling in eighty languages, and only Nuh could communicate with all of them.

The post Isma'il language is called *al-'Arabiyya* (Arabiyya), and *al-'Arabiyya al-Mubina* (accessible Arabiyya), and *al-'Arabiyya al-Fasiha* (lucid Arabiyya) and *al-'Arabiyya al-Hanifiyya* (the monotheists' Arabiyya), which stress the modernity, the flexibility and the religious dimension of the new Arabiyya that has survived to the present day.

The Arabiyya has flourished as a rich and dynamic language since the time of the Prophet Muhammad (570-632), and there is no reason why it could not have prospered from the time of Isma'il to the time of his descendant the Prophet Muhammad. The Qur'an, the Hadith, the diversity of Jahili literature, and the extensive and wideranging vocabulary reflecting every aspect of Jahili urban, country and *bedu* life, support this view. The fact that the Arabian Peninsula has never experienced invasions or waves of foreign migrations helped it preserve its way of life and its language, and develop unique literary forms, metrical and rhyming patterns, and poetic conventions, which became the hallmark of Arab, Persian, Ottoman and Urdu literatures.

It is interesting to note that Arabists think that the Arabiyya of Jahiliyya is a cocktail of Aramaic, Hebrew, Greek, Syriac, Latin and Persian, mixed and shaken round about two or three centuries before Islam. What is surprising is that these scholars seem to have overlooked the fact that the Arabiyya of Jahiliyya is far more developed and complex than the languages from which it supposedly evolved.

The Arabiyya of Jahiliyya shares certain characteristics with Ugaritic, a language which is as old if not older than Aramaic, Hebrew, Greek, Syriac, Latin and Persian. For example, one of Allah's attributes *Assamad* (Eternal, Powerful), which was thought to be an exclusively Arab word, is also one of the attributes of the major Ugaritic god El. Other attributes of Allah like *Assalaam* (Perfect, whole, Peace) and *Alhannaan* (Merciful, Loving) are also attributes of El.

As nothing was known about the Ugaritic civilisation since its demise in 250 BCE until the 1930s, how did these attributes crop up in Arabiyya? Was Arabiyya influenced by Ugaritic? Or was Ugaritic influenced by Arabiyya? As Ugaritic had been dead and forgotten for over a thousand years before the presumed birth of Arabiyya, it is inconceivable that it could have had an impact on Arabiyya. On the other hand, the similarities unique to Ugaritic and Arabiyya would indicate that the two languages were contemporaneous and shared a common cultural origin.

V

The Religions of Jahiliyya

The diversity of the Jahili civilisations produced various religions, with each tribal region having its own god or gods or other forms of worship through which it communicated with Allah the Creator of the Universe. First, there were those who believed in Allah, in the resurrection and the hereafter, and in the reward for the pious and the punishment for the sinner. Second, there were those who believed in Allah, the resurrection and the hereafter but not in the prophets. Third, there were those who believed in Allah but not in the resurrection nor in the prophets; they believed in the concept of time which would eventually destroy mankind. Fourth, there were those who believed in angels whom they regarded as the daughters of Allah from His marriage to the genii. Fifth, there were those who believed in the genii. Sixth, there were those who rejected the concept of the Creator and the resurrection. Seventh, there were those who believed in the Christian faith. Eighth, there were those who believed in the Jewish faith. Ninth, there were those who believed in the Persian Mazdaki creed. Tenth, there were those who worshipped Venus, the sun, the moon, Jupiter, Sirius, Canopus, Mercury and Taurus. The sun was known as *ilaha*, which is the feminine form of *ilah* (god on high).

Tradition relates that Allah was the One and Only God worshipped in the Ka‘ba. The prophets Ibrahim and Isma‘il reintroduced the Hanif (monotheist) religion based on the Oneness of Allah. The Hanif religion continued to thrive up to the time ‘Amr b. Luhayy set up idols in the Ka‘ba as intermediaries between man and Allah. The introduction of idol worship curtailed the influence of the Hanif religion which re-emerged before the rise of Islam as an alternative to the intercessionary religions. The Hanifs were ruthlessly persecuted by the Qurashi intercessionists who had been the custodians of the Ka'ba since the fifth century CE. One of the most prominent Hanifs (monotheists) was the prophet Khalid b. Sinan who walked into the centre of the firebelching cave and miraculously extinguished the *Fire of al-Harratain* with his stick, thereby putting a stop to the fire worship that had been going on since Qaabeel's (Cain's) time.

The Prophet Muhammad held the Hanifs in high esteem, and their teachings are echoed in the Qur'an's early Meccan *suras*. This is evident from "*Surat al-Ikhlas": Qul Huwa Allahu Ahad...lam yalid wa lam yulad* (Say Allah is the One and Only God... He neither procreates nor was He procreated), which crystallises the essence of Khalid b. Sinan's concept of Allah: *Huwa Allahu Wahid, laisa bimawlud wala walid* (Allah is the One and Only God, He neither procreates nor was He procreated). When Khalid b. Sinan's daughter heard the Prophet reciting "*Surat al-Ikhlas*" she said: "O Messenger of Allah, this is what my father used to say." The Prophet agreed with her and praised her father: "He was a prophet lost by his people."

Throughout his preaching life the Prophet Muhammad stressed that Islam was not a new religion but the continuation of the Hanif religion Ibrahim and his son Isma'il inherited from Adam and his son Hibatullah (Seth). The Prophet Muhammad regarded the Jahilis as monotheists who believed in Allah as the One and Only God, but over the centuries they distorted their faith by introducing other deities and worshipping them as intermediaries between themselves and Allah. The Prophet Muhammad maintained that the introduction of the intermediary deities corrupted the original message of Ibrahim and Isma'il, which was subsequently restored by Islam.

When the Prophet Muhammad took Mecca he went straight to the Ka'ba, which the Jahilis had turned into a pantheon for their gods, and destroyed the statues of three hundred and sixty gods. Among the three hundred and sixty idols placed around the Ka'ba were the statues of Ibrahim and Isma'il holding the oracle arrows. And in the Ka'ba were frescoes of scenes dominated by the figures of Ibrahim, Isma'il, 'Isa (Jesus), Mariam (Mary) and the angels. And on the door of the Ka'ba were the brassencased horns of Jareer, the sheep Ibrahim sacrificed in place of Isma'il. The horns remained on the door of the Ka'ba until the Ka'ba was destroyed during the siege of Mecca by the forces of the Umayyad Caliph 'Abd al-Malik b. Marwan (646-705).

The presence of the figures of Ibrahim, Isma'il, 'Isa and Mariam in the Ka'ba implies: either the Ka'ba had become the centre of worship for the Arab Jews and the Arab Christians, or these figures were part of the Jahili mythological worship which had nothing to do with the Judaeo-Christian tradition. As the Ka'ba was the centre of worship for the Arabs and had no Judaeo-Christian terms of reference, and housed many gods who were anathema to Jews and Christians, it is unthinkable that the Arab Jews and the Arab Christians would use the Ka'ba as a place of worship. Therefore, the presence of the above figures in the Ka'ba had no Judaeo-Christian relevance and formed part of the Jahili mythological tradition, which is as old as the history of man in the Arabian Peninsula.

Inspite of centuries of preaching by Jews and Christians in the Arabian Peninsula, Judaism and Christianity failed to make substantial inroads among the Jahilis, even though the two religions had, at different periods, strong political and military support. The Jahili Jewish tribes of Arabia were essentially Arabs who were converted to Judaism by various means: intermarriages, theological persuasion, political expediency and force. Although the Qahtani king of Yemen Dhu Nuwas (d. 524), a convert to Judaism, used force to Judaicise the Qahtani Christian community of the South Arabian kingdom of Najran, the Jews, on the whole, stayed aloof from their non-Jewish neighbours, and maintained only business contact. By the way, the Jahili Jewish tribes of Arabia are not mentioned in the Hebrew sources, and the information on them comes primarily from Arab tradition.

In the case of Christianity, the Jahilis saw it as another intercessionary religion whose idea of Jesus as the son of God paralleled their concept of the three goddesses Allat, al-'Uzza and Manat as the daughters of Allah. Moreover, the notion that the intercessionary gods could be killed by human hands exists in Jahili and Christian religions. Just as Jesus was killed by human hands, so was the Jahili god Nasr who, before his death, used to visit his earthly worshippers once a year to tell them what to do in the coming year.

There is no record of the Hebrew Torah and the Gospels being translated into Arabiyya in Jahiliyya, nor is it likely that they had been translated. For if the two books had been available in Arabiyya, their influence would have been apparent in Jahili literature, at least in the works of the Jewish and Christian writers. But there is hardly any Judaeo-Christian influence in Jahili literature, nor in the literature of the Islam and Umayyad periods.

According to the Encyclopaedia Judaica the first Arabiyya translation of the Hebrew Torah written in Hebrew characters for the benefit of Arab Jews was by the Abbasid Jewish theologian Sa'adia Ga'on (882-942), though extracts from the

Hebrew Torah in Arabiyya were already in circulation before Sa'adia's version. The pre Sa 'adia Arabiyya version of the Hebrew Torah could well be the work of Ahmad b. Abdullah b. Salam, who was a protégé of the Caliph Harun al-Rashid (763-809) and who, according to the bibliographer Ibn al-Nadim (d. 1000), translated the Hebrew Torah and the Gospels into Arabiyya. In addition, Hebrew had ceased to be a day-to-day language for a few centuries before the Prophet Muhammad's time, and was confined to the synagogue. In fact, the revival of Hebrew happened under the Arab cultural shadow long after the advent of Islam.

On the other hand, the language of the Jahili Jews and Christians was Arabiyya which drew on a long and uninterrupted Arab literary and religious tradition. Also, the Jahilis had their own scriptures, prayer and devotional books such as *Kitab Allah* (The Book of Allah) and *Kitab al-Talbiya* (The Book of Talbiya Prayers), and many Jahili religious expressions permeate current speech. For this reason the Qur'an and the Hadith should be read against a Jahili background rather than against a Judaeo-Christian setting. After all, the Qur'an and the Hadith were addressed to the Jahilis who were familiar with the idiom and the terms of reference of the two works. Even the Jahili children found the Qur'an accessible to the extent that the Prophet Muhammad's detractors thought he was a storyteller rehashing old yarns. And this accounts for the Prophet's success in Islamising the Arabian Peninsula in twenty years. Incidentally, the Qur'an was revealed not only to show the Jahilis the path of Islam, but as a unique literary work that challenged the established literary forms and conventions. Indeed, the Jahilis were taken by the Qur'an's unusual language, form and style, though they could not make out whether the Qur'an was poetry or prose, because the Qur'an did not fit in with any of their poetic and prose genres.

There were several Ka'bas in the Arabian Peninsula, but the oldest and most important was the Meccan Ka'ba, which was the Jahilis' centre of worship, where they prayed and went round it seven times. The Jahilis went on pilgrimage to the Meccan Ka'ba once a year. The pilgrimage season lasted for a week, and alternated between the month of Dhu al-Qa'da for two successive years and the month of Dhu al-Hijja for two successive years. The last time the Prophet Muhammad went on pilgrimage happened to be in the month of Dhu al-Hijja, and from then on the Prophet decided that the pilgrimage season should always be in the month of Dhu al-Hijja.

In the Ka'ba pantheon were the goddesses Allat, al-'Uzza and Manat, who occupied a special place in the hearts of the Jahilis. The three goddesses were worshipped as the daughters of Allah, and represented three different aspects of Allah. Allat is the feminine form of Allah, and she is the goddess of love and fertility. Al-'Uzza is the feminine form of al-A'azz, which means al-'Aziz (Noble and All-powerful), and she is the goddess of power, love and beauty. Al-'Uzza is the Arab Venus who resided in three gumacacia trees that grew in her temple. Manat is the feminine form of Mana (Allah's Will), and she is the goddess of fate.

One of the intercessionary prayers dedicated to the three goddesses runs:

> *wa Allati wa al-'Uzza, wa Manata al-Thalithati al-Ukhra, fa innahunna al-Gharaniqu al-Ula, wa inna Shafa'atahunna la turtaja.*

> (By Allat and al-'Uzza, and by the third one Manat, the beautiful and the exalted ones, whose intercession is sought.)

The intercessionary prayer of the three goddesses, which the members of the Qurashi tribe chanted as they circumambulated the Ka'ba, was picked up by the Prophet Muhammad's detractors who used it to throw doubt on the divine source of the Prophet's revelation.

The story goes that while the Prophet was in a revelationary state in the mosque Iblees (Satan) put in his mouth the Qurashi intercessionary prayer as revelationary *ayas* (verses), and then informed the intercessionists present in the mosque that the Prophet had acknowledged the intermediary significance of their goddesses Allat, al-'Uzza and Manat. Iblees's message pleased the intercessionists and so they prayed together with the Muslims. Initially the Muslims were glad to see the intercessionists praying with them; but when they were told why the intercessionists were praying with them they were upset by what they thought the Prophet had done. The angel Jibreel joined the chorus of disapproval and told the Prophet: "You have uttered words I did not bring you from Allah." The Prophet then recanted the Ibleesian *ayas* (Satanic verses) and published a revised version which appears in the Qur'an in *Surat al-Najm*:

> *Afa ra'aitumu Allata wa al-'Uzza, wa Manata al-Thalithata al-Ukhra, alakumu al-Dhakaru wa lahu al-Untha, tilka idhan qismatun diza.*
>
> (See how you thought of Allat and al-'Uzza, and the third one Manat: you have made yourself the father of

> boys and made Him the father of girls. But this is a twisted choice.)

The argument of the Prophet's detractors that the relevant *ayas* in *Surat al-Najm* are a revised version of the "Satanic verses" falls apart on close examination. Firstly, as the Prophet was a Qurashi well versed in Jahili culture, who must have obviously been familiar with the Qurashi intercessionary prayer, it is inconceivable that he would have endorsed such an intercessionary prayer which is inconsistent with the essence of the message of Islam. Secondly, had the Prophet presented the Qurashi intercessionary prayer as revelationary *ayas*, he would have lost his credibility as the Messenger of Allah, and Islam would have ended up as another intercessionary religion. Thirdly, the rhythmic structure of the Qurashi intercessionary prayer is different from that of the relevant *ayas* and from the rest of the *ayas* in *Surat al-Najm*, and there is not a single discordant *aya* in the Qur'an. Fourthly, semantically the Qurashi intercessionary prayer and the relevant *ayas* say two different things in two different forms of speech: the Qurashi intercessionary prayer is a statement of fact, whereas the relevant *ayas* are argumentative and more in line with the tone of the *ayas* that precede them and of the *ayas* that follow them in *Surat al-Najm*. Fifthly, since the Qur'an was revealed to the Prophet through Jibreel, there was no way for Iblees to reach the Prophet in a revelationary state except by overpowering Jibreel, but the "Satanic" episode makes no reference to a Jibreel-Iblees encounter; indeed, Jibreel was just as surprised as everyone else by what the Prophet was thought to have done. Sixthly, the fact that the Muslims were upset only after they had been told what the Prophet said, and that the intercessionists prayed with the Muslims only after Iblees had informed them of the Prophet's endorsement of their three goddesses means either the Muslim and the intercessionist congregations were stone deaf or the Prophet did not utter the "Satanic verses"; and if this had been the case then the whole "Satanic" episode would be no more than a teasing apocryphal tale.

One of the most important gods in the Ka'ba was Hubal, whose name recalls the name of Adam's son Haabeel (Abel). The statue of Hubal was of red cornelian in the shape of a tall, wise man with a long beard, and his broken right hand had been replaced with a gold hand by the Qurashis. Hubal held in his right hand seven oracle arrows, and each arrow was marked for each day of the week.

The Jahilis kept images of their family gods in their homes. Members of the family who intended to travel sought the blessing of the family god by touching his image, and the same ritual was repeated on their return.

In *Kitab al-Asnam* (The Book of Idols) the Arab mythologist Ibn al-Kalbi (d. 819) traces the origins of five of the major Jahili gods: Wadd, Siwaa', Yaghooth, Ya'ooq and Nasr. In the distant past there were five virtuous men called Wadd, Siwaa', Yaghooth, Ya'ooq and Nasr. When they died their families were griefstricken. Iblees assumed the appearance of a man from the Banu Qaabeel, who were the descendants of Adam's son Qaabeel (Cain), and approached the aggrieved families and offered to make statues resembling the five deceased. The families agreed. Iblees carved five statues out of stone which looked like the deceased and exhibited them. When the relatives saw the statues of their dead they were so impressed by them that they addressed them respectfully while going round them. This ritual was performed for a century, and in the following century the statues were held in higher esteem than in the previous century. In the third century people thought their predecessors venerated the statues in the belief that the statues were intermediaries between themselves and Allah. As a result the statues acquired greater importance. This idol worship displeased Allah Who sent the prophet Idris (Enoch) to show the people the right path. But the people ignored Idris's message and continued to worship the five idols until the time of the prophet Nuh who was then four hundred years old. For one hundred and twenty years Nuh entreated his people to worship Allah as the One and Only God. But when Allah saw that Nuh was not making any progress He instructed him to build the Ark. By the time he finished building the Ark Nuh was six hundred years old. Then Allah flooded the earth. In the Flood the five statues drifted about until they were swept ashore in Jeddah and the wind buried them in the sand.

'Amr b. Luhayy was a kahin (priest) who lived in Tihama and was in touch with a genie called Abu Thumama who was his ra'i (seer). One day the genie urged 'Amr to go to Jeddah to bring the statues of Wadd, Siwaa', Yaghooth, Ya'ooq and Nasr to Tihama, then call on all the Arabs to worship them. 'Amr travelled to the river of Jeddah, dug up the five buried statues and brought them to Tihama. During the Hajj (pilgrimage) season 'Amr took the five statues to Mecca and called on all the Arabs to worship them, and all the Arabs responded to his call. The five idols were worshipped until the advent of Islam.

Tradition has it that Wadd, Siwaa', Yaghooth, Ya'ooq and Nasr were the sons of Adam. Another tradition maintains that Wadd was the son of Qaabeel, Siwaa' the son of Wadd, Yaghooth the son of Siwaa', Ya'ooq the son of Yaghooth, and Nasr the son of Ya'ooq. But the two traditions agree that the five gods lived before Idris (Enoch).

The statue of Wadd (love, mountain) was of gigantic proportions and wore two garments, one was wrapped round his waist and the other covered the rest of his body. He wore a sword, had a bow across his shoulder, a twisted spear with a standard in one hand and a pouch full of arrows in the other hand. One of the attributes of Allah is Wadud, which is the adjectival form of Wadd. The appearance and the name of Wadd suggest that Wadd represented the Loving and Allpowerful aspects of Allah. The name of the god Wadd, which is short for Wadad, brings to mind the name of the Hebrew king David (beloved) but in a metathesised form.

Some of the Jahilis believed that the blood and the soul are one and the same. When someone was killed the bloodsoul came out of the head of the deceased as a male owl called *Sada* if the deceased was a man or as a female owl called *Haama* if the deceased was a woman, and perched on the grave of the deceased, screeching: "Give me a drink! Give me a drink!" until the deceased was avenged. But if the deceased died of natural causes the *Sada* owl or the *Haama* owl would live with the family of the deceased and report news about the family to the deceased for a hundred years. The bloodsoul belief is encapsulated in the Jahili expression *salat nafsuhu* (his soul flowed away) which is still used in current speech.

Other Jahilis believed that the soul was a bird residing in the body, and when the body expired the birdsoul, like the bloodsoul, came out of the head of the deceased as a *Sada* owl or as a *Haama* owl and performed the same rituals as the bloodsoul owls. The birdsoul belief is embodied in the everyday expression *tarat ruhuhu* (his soul flew away).

The Jahilis called the grave *Bait al-Haqq* (The House of Truth). It was the custom of the Jahilis to wash the dead body, wrap it in a shroud and pray for the deceased, then carry the body on a pall to the cemetery. Before the burial, the family of the deceased recounted the good qualities of the deceased and ended by saying: *'Alaik rahmat Allah* (May Allah welcome you with Forgiveness and Love). The family of the deceased would leave a *Baliyya* camel (The Camel of the Dead) tied to the grave of the deceased without food or drink, for it was believed that on the day of the resurrection the deceased would rise and ride the camel to the Judgement Centre to be judged and then sent either to paradise or hell. The Jahilis talked to their dead so as to deny the fact that their loved ones were really dead, and to keep their memory alive. The Jahilis also used to say before starting on anything: "*Bism Allah*" (By the Blessing of Allah), which is short for *Bism Allah Arrahman Arrahim* (By the Blessing of Allah, the Merciful Lord of Forgiveness and Love).

The Jahilis followed the lunar calendar which is of three hundred and fifty four days, whereas the solar calendar is of three hundred and sixty five days. But since the Jahilis believed in astral worship and that the stars controlled the seasons and the rains, it was important that the lunar months should coincide with the appearance of the relevant stars. The Jahilis solved this problem by having a leap year of thirteen months every three years which bridged the gap between the lunar and the solar calendars. The fixed lunar calendar was disrupted by the Prophet Muhammad who cancelled the leap year, so that the lunar months would not coincide with the appearance of the relevant stars. By so doing the Prophet terminated astral worship.

One of the astral gods worshipped by the Jahilis was Canopus who was originally a tax collector turned into a star by Allah as a punishment for overtaxing merchants. The myth of Canopus says that Canopus married Gemini and while he was consummating the marriage he broke her backbone. Fearing the retribution of the gods, Canopus crossed the Milky Way and ran away to Yemen. Sirius, who was in love with

Canopus, crossed the Milky Way and followed Canopus, leaving behind her sister Procyon in tears, who was also in love with Canopus but unable to cross the Milky Way.

VI

The Arab Genesis

Over the centuries we have been conditioned to assume the Hebrew Genesis as the source of all the Genesis stories circulating in the Arab world. And only the discovery of the Sumerian, Babylonian, Egyptian and Ugaritic myths of creation freed us from this misconception. Future excavations in Arabia will undoubtedly unearth more creation myths predating the Hebrew Genesis.

If the Arab and Jewish traditions are true that Ibrahim (Abraham) was a historical figure, and was the progenitor of Isma'il (Ishmael) and Isaac, the patriarchs of the Arabs and the Jews, and that the two sons adopted their father's faith, then the Genesis lore must obviously belong to both the Arabs and the Jews. The joint ownership of the Genesis lore leads to the conclusion that an Arab Genesis exists alongside the Hebrew Genesis. The general outline of the Arab and Hebrew Genesis stories confirms this view, though the stories differ in emphasis and detail, as can be gauged from the following examples.

First example:

> The Arab Genesis relates that when Ibrahim's firstborn and only son Isma'il was in his early teens Allah asked Ibrahim to sacrifice him as a test of his faith in Him. Ibrahim took Isma'il to Jabal Mina in Mecca and as he was about to sacrifice him, Allah said to Ibrahim: "Your willingness to sacrifice your firstborn and only son is a strong proof of your unshakeable faith." In appreciation Allah gave

Ibrahim Haabeel's (Abel's) lamb Jareer, which Allah had kept in paradise to be sacrificed in place of Isma'il.

Second example:

The Arab Genesis relates that before building the Ka'ba, Ibrahim flew the *Buraq* (a mythical, quadrupede, winged creature with a human head) with Jibreel to the seventh heaven Raqee. While he was in the seventh heaven Raqee, Ibrahim looked down at the earth and pointed at the remains of the foundations of the Ka'ba and said to Jibreel: "I would like to build Allah's House the Ka'ba on those ruins." Jibreel said: "You have chosen the same spot on which Adam built Allah's House the Ka'ba." Ibrahim returned to earth and went to Mecca guided by the Sakina (the Spirit of Allah that takes different forms, one of which is a winged, ethereal creature with a human face) that hovered like a cloud above him all the way to the Ka'ba grounds. The Sakina then threw a shadow over the ruins on the Ka'ba grounds and said to Ibrahim: "Ibrahim, build Allah's House the Ka'ba on the ruins under My Shadow." And Ibrahim rebuilt the Ka'ba with his son Isma'il who was twenty years old.

In the Hebrew Genesis there is no mention of the Ka'ba, and Isaac is the object of sacrifice, and the ram sacrificed in his place is not associated with Abel.

Third example:

The Arab Genesis relates that before Nuh boarded the Ark with his eighty companions, he appealed to his son Yaam

> to believe in Allah and join him in the Ark before Allah flooded the earth. Yaam ignored Nuh's appeals and said that should Allah flood the earth he would seek refuge in one of the mountains. Nuh assured Yaam that it would not be long before the mountains and the rest of the earth would be submerged in water. Yaam ignored his father's pleas. Allah flooded the earth and Yaam perished in the Flood.

Fourth example:

> Allah sent Nuh a black bead and a white bead so Nuh could distinguish night from day in the floating Ark. During the day the light of the white bead overwhelmed the darkness of the black bead, and during the night the darkness of the black bead overwhelmed the light of the white bead.

In the Hebrew Genesis there is no reference to Yaam (rt. ymm) nor to the eighty passengers, and the only human passengers Noah had with him were his wife and his three sons Shem, Ham and Japheth and their wives. Besides, there is no reference to the white and black beads; instead, God instructed Noah to make an opening in the Ark so he could tell night from day.

It is worth noting the connection of Yaam with the Flood, because in Ugaritic mythology Yaam was the god of the sea. The word *yamm* denotes 'sea' in Arabiyya, Ugaritic, and Hebrew, as well as being a Jahili proper name: Yaam b. Asba al-Hamdani of the Banu Kahlan, and Yaam b. 'Ans b. Madhhij of the Banu Kahlan and Zarqa al-Yamama. The two Yaams, who trace their descent to Qahtan (Joktan) b. Hud b. 'Abir (Eber), are the patriarchs of the Yaam tribes still prospering in Yemen. *Yamm* also means serpent and evokes other associations which are probably rooted in the ancient rituals of the sea god Yaam, such as *amma* (to seek the straight path), *mi'amm* (guide), *yamam* (turtle dove), *imam* (religious leader) and the *tayammum* ablution which is still practised by Muslims to this day. The Christian baptismal rites may also have Yaamian echoes. The plight of Nuh's drowned son Yaam is summed up in the Jahili proverb *Innama haam 'Ammuna Yaam* (Our uncle Yaam wandered off and got lost). The cultural nuances of *yamm* are further evidence of the continuity of the Arab tradition since the Nuh Flood.

There are two questions concerning the Jahili Yaam tribes that come to mind: Did the Jahili Yaam tribes worship the sea god Yaam? And if they did, was the Arabian sea god Yaam an Ugaritic import or an Arabian export? The answers to these questions probably lay buried in the land of Yaam or in some manuscripts waiting to be discovered.

Some classical Arab lexicographers held that the word *yamm* was borrowed from Hebrew without justifying their claim. If this is true then words like *'ain* (eye, spring), *ra's* (head), *bait* (house) and so on, must have been borrowed from the Arabiyya related languages, such as Hebrew, Aramaic, Akkadian, Canaanite, Ugaritic, Phoenician, Assyrian, Ethiopic and Syriac, because these languages have the same words. But these words, like many Arabiyya words, are common to the Arabiyya related languages, and there is nothing to indicate that such words evolved out of a particular culture. Moreover, our knowledge of the ancient civilisations of the Arab World is limited and essentially speculative. The word *yamm*, therefore, is no more of a loan word than the words that are common to the languages related to Arabiyya.

It should be pointed out that the classical Arab lexicographers who advanced the theory of the non-Arab origin of some of the Arabiyya words, especially those in the Qur'an, were not conversant with the languages from which the

Arabiyya words they claimed originated. The etymological studies of the Arabiyya words of the last two hundred years are just as flawed as those of the classical period, because these studies, like all Arab and Islam studies, are not founded on a thorough investigation of the discipline concerned, but on footnote, index, luckydip and informant scholarship. The reason for this flawed scholarship is that most Arabists, if not all, come from different cultural backgrounds and lack the essential qualification, which is a command of Arabiyya, nor are they sufficiently drilled in the mechanics of their own languages and literatures. So the attempts of such scholars to trace the Arabiyya words to other languages are purely conjectural and tell us more about the conjecturers and their dappling scholarship than about the words themselves.

As there are linguistic affinities between Arabiyya and its related languages, due to their common origin, it is inevitable that the myths of the related peoples should also reflect a common source rather than the influence of one tradition upon another tradition.

The same thing can be said about Arab mythology and the Arabiyya words thought to be of Greek and Persian origin, as the Greek and Persian languages and mythologies were influenced by the Arabiyya and the Arabiyya related languages and mythologies. For example, after the fall of Babylon to the Persians in 539 BCE, the Persians used Aramaic as their official language until the Persian empire was destroyed by Alexander the Great in 331 BCE. The reliance of the Persians on Aramaic for so long means that ancient Persian was not fully developed to cope with the linguistic needs of an empire and an urban society. During its dominant role as an official language, Aramaic must have had a profound impact on the development of ancient Persian and Pahlavi (Middle Persian) in a way similar to that of the Arabiyya on Modern Persian. The writing down of the Persian religious texts in the sixth century CE and of the Persian myths of creation, eschatology and apocalyptic literature in the ninth and tenth centuries CE, and the flowering of Pahlavi thought and literature also in the ninth and tenth centuries CE, are further evidence of the slow development of ancient and Pahlavi Persian in general and Persian intellectual life in particular.

In the eighth and ninth centuries CE a number of Shu'ubi (anti-Arab) writers published a series of books in Arabiyya and passed them off as translations from Pahlavi works written in the sixth century CE. But when the Shu'ubi writers were challenged by their contemporary critics to produce the unheard of Pahlavi originals, they were unable to do so, and were thus accused of fabricating the nonexisting Pahlavi titles. The critics argued that the socalled translated books could not have been translations from the sixth century Pahlavi, but were original works written in Arabiyya, because the form, style, theme, syntactical structure and terms of reference of these works betray a strong Arab background. And to this day no Pahlavi originals have surfaced to verify the Shu'ubi writers' claim. The Arabiyya works were subsequently translated into Modern Persian, which suggests there were no Pahlavi originals.

As the Pahlavi world was articulated under the Arab cultural umbrella in the Abbasid period, it is not surprising to find Arab elements in Persian mythology, eschatology and apocalyptic literature. Indeed, the debt of the Persians to the Arabs was recognised as early as the fifth century BCE by the Greek historian Herodotus (485-425 BCE) who says that the Persian Mithra cult was influenced by the Arabian Alilat (Allat/Aphrodite) cult.

It is important to remember that the whole area from Iraq to the Mediterranean was one cultural unit whose centre kept on changing at different times from one region to another region: from Iraq to Yemen, to Syria, to Egypt, to Crete, to Greece and to Rome. The recent deciphering of the Minoan script called Linear A proves that the Minoans were of Musnad origin, and shows how closely related were the ancient civilisations.

The one area that has so far not been excavated as extensively as Egypt and Iraq is the Arabian Peninsula. It is hoped that future excavations in Arabia will yield the full text of the Arab Genesis that has survived in fragmentary form in the Qur'an, the Hadith, classical and folk literature. *The Arab Creation* Myth is a reconstruction of the Arab Genesis based on the surviving fragments.

In the meantime, while waiting for the Arab Genesis to turn up to take us back to the mythological domain of the Jahilis, let us explore the Jahili world through *The Arab Creation Myth*.

THE ARAB CREATION MYTH

TALBIYA PRAYERS

1

Labbaik, O Lord, Labbaik.

2

Labbaik, O Merciful Lord of Forgiveness and Love.

3

Labbaik, O Magnanimous Lord of Patience and Hope.

4

Labbaik, O Lord of the Throne, of the Pen and the Lawh, of Revelation and Dreams, and of the Sacred Houses Duraah, Bait Ma'moor and the Ka'ba.

5

Labbaik, O Lord of paradise and hell, of the celestial and Bain regions, of Illiyyeen and the Shields, and of the heavens and the earths and the sky.

6

Labbaik, O Lord of the heavenly and earthly seas, of the seven seas and the skysea, of the Masjoor Sea and the seven seas of fire.

7

Labbaik, O Lord of the sun and the moon, of the Khunnas planets and the stars, of the comets and the Milky Way.

8

Labbaik, O Lord of the barrier of darkness, of darkness and light, of night and day.

9

Labbaik, O Lord of the eclipse and the rainbow, of East and West, of North and South.

10

Labbaik, O Lord of the mountains, the wadis and the hills, of meadows and plains, of deserts and horizons.

11

Labbaik, O Lord of the roads and the bridges, of soil and sand, and of rocks, pebbles and stones.

12

Labbaik, O Lord of the clouds, of thunder and lightning, of volcanoes and fuel, and of the winds, fire and air.

13

Labbaik, O Lord of water and rain, of dew and snow, of rivers and lakes, and of streams, wells and springs.

14

Labbaik, O Lord of plants and trees, of fields, gardens and woods, and of the seasons, colours and flowers.

15

Labbaik, O Lord of the angels, the genii and Man, and of the paradisial, heavenly and earthly creatures.

16

Labbaik, O Lord of the fish of the heavenly and earthly seas, of the fish of the seven seas and the skysea.

17

Labbaik, O Lord of the earthly birds and beasts, and of those who walk and those who ride.

18

Labbaik, O Compassionate Lord of the living and the dead, of joy and grief and Retribution.

19

Labbaik, O Lord of the secrets of the heart, of the permissible and the prohibited.

20

Labbaik, O Lord of the Infinite, Lord of Eternal Life.

21

Labbaik, O Lord of Wisdom, the Allseeing, the Allknowing, the Allpowerful, Our Guide to Eternal Life.

22

Labbaik, Our One and Only worshipped Lord, Lord of the Worlds, Lord of All Creation.

SURA ONE

The Vision

1

Allah was on a cloud.

2

Allah looked above the cloud and saw nothing, not even air.

3

Allah looked under the cloud and saw nothing, not even air.

4

Allah explored the emptiness around Him for two thousand years and saw nothing, not even air.

5

Allah reflected: "There is scope for this space."

6

So Allah thought of creating the world.

SURA TWO

The Creation of the Throne, the Pen and the Lawh

1

Allah perceived a Throne, and then created the Throne from His Own Light.

2

Allah gazed at the Throne and thought: "This Throne will be My Throne, and from the Light of My Throne I will create the world to fill this space."

3

Allah created a white pearl from the Light of His Throne.

4

Out of the white pearl Allah created the Pen, the Pen was as long as the distance from earth to heaven and as wide as a distance of eighty years.

5

A thousand years after the creation of the Pen, Allah created a white pearl from the Light of His Throne.

6

Out of the white pearl Allah created the Lawh, the Lawh was as long as the distance from earth to heaven and as wide as the distance from east to west.

7

One side of the Lawh was a stretched ruby and the other side of the Lawh was a stretched emerald.

8

Allah stared intently at the Pen, and luminous ink dripdropped from the nib of the Pen.

9

Allah said to the Pen: "Write on the Lawh."

10

The Pen said: "Lord, what shall I write on the Lawh?"

11

Allah said: "Write down My Creation Plan and what is going to happen from now until the end of time, the time I am about to create."

12

The Pen said: "Labbaik, O Lord of All Creation."

13

Allah sat on His Throne and spent fifty thousand years drawing up His Creation Plan.

SURA THREE

The Creation of Heaven and Earth, the Wind and the Soor

1

Allah created a green gem many times the size of the heavens and the earths from the Light of His Throne.

2

Allah stared intently at the green gem which melted and turned into water.

3

Allah created the wind from His Own Breath and let the water flow on the surface of the wind.

4

Allah got up and placed His Throne on the water, sat on the Throne and stared intently at the water.

5

Fear shot through the water and made it boil.

6

Smoke and foam began to rise from the water.

7

Out of the smoke Allah created heaven and divided heaven into seven heavens, and separated each heaven from the next heaven by a distance of five hundred years, and each heaven had a density of a distance of five hundred years.

8

Out of the foam Allah created the earth and kept the earth at a distance of five hundred years from heaven, and divided the earth into seven earths, and separated each earth from the next earth by a distance of five hundred years, and each earth had a density of a distance of five hundred years.

9

And out of the wind Allah created the air and the breeze and the seven winds: the South Wind, the North Wind, the East Wind, the West Wind, the Nabka Wind, the Kharooq Wind and the Qaa'im Wind, and each of the seven winds had two wings and a tail.

10

Allah created a pearl from the Light of His Throne.

11

Out of the pearl Allah created the Soor, and the Soor was in the shape of a round oven, and was as transparent as glass and had as many beehivelike holes as there were living creatures, and in the beehivelike holes nested the souls of the dead, and in the middle of the Soor was the largest of the beehivelike holes, which was the size of the seven heavens and the seven earths; and at the appointed hour the Soor would be blown thrice, signalling the end of time, and the nesting souls of the dead would come out of the beehivelike holes glowing.

SURA FOUR

The Creation of the Seas, the Plants and the Animals

1

Allah created the seven heavenly seas, the seven earthly seas, the seven seas, the plants, the animals and other creatures out of water, and populated the seven heavenly seas and the seven earthly seas and the seven seas with plants and fish and other sea creatures, and the seven earths with plants and animals and other earthly creatures, and the seven earths had forty thousand species of earthly creatures, and the seven earthly seas had forty thousand species of sea creatures.

2

Each of the seven heavenly seas and of the seven earthly seas and of the seven seas had a depth of a distance of five hundred years.

3

Each heavenly sea was placed between one heaven and another heaven, and each earthly sea was placed between one earth and another earth.

4

The seventh heavenly sea, which had still waves like an extended mountain and ran like an arrow shot in the air or like a string stretched from east to west, met the seventh earthly sea and both seas filled the distance that separated the first heaven from the first earth.

5

Allah parted the seventh heavenly sea from the seventh earthly sea, and inbetween Allah put the sky and the skysea, which He created out of the overspilt waters of the seventh heavenly sea and the seventh earthly sea, and the skysea was a fifteen-kilometre spread of still waves below the sky and had as many plants and fish as the seven heavenly seas and the seven earthly seas.

SURA FIVE

The Creation of Paradise and the Angels

1

Allah created paradise from the Light of His Throne and divided paradise into seven paradises, and each paradise was made of a hundred regions, and each paradisial region was separated from the next paradisial region by a distance of five hundred years.

2

The paradisial regions were so unbelievably vast that each of them could easily absorb the seven heavens and the seven earths.

3

The first paradisial region was the colour of silver, the second paradisial region was the colour of gold, the third paradisial region was the colour of emeralds, rubies and pearls, and the remaining ninety seven paradisial regions were in colours that had never been seen by human eyes, nor heard of by human ears, nor perceived by human minds.

4

The seven paradises were surrounded by four paradisial walls of gold and silver bricks, and each paradisial wall had the thickness of a distance of forty years.

5

The seven paradises had eight gates, and each paradisial gate, which was kept at a distance of seventy years from the gate of the next paradise and had a rubyring knocker framed in gold, consisted of two gateleaves whose width spanned a distance of eighty years.

6

The first paradisial gate was called Baab Tawba and the remaining seven paradisial gates were named after their respective paradises.

7

Allah made the seven paradises breathe, and out of the seven paradises' breath Allah created the only paradisial season: the Eternal Spring.

8

The seven paradises breathed the flowerscented Spring Breath to sustain the paradisians.

9

Allah created the angels from the Light of His Throne and put them in the seven paradises and in the seven heavens to worship Him, and then populated the seven paradises with plants, animals and other paradisial creatures He created out of water.

10

The seven paradises had refreshing and muskscented rivers, streams and springs, and along the banks of the paradisial rivers, streams and springs were gold and silver cups.

11

The seven paradises had trees whose scented flowers and fruit had never been seen by human eyes nor heard of by human ears nor perceived by human minds, and whenever the paradisial scented flowers and fruit were picked, new scented flowers and fruit grew instantly in their place.

12

The first paradise was Jannat Jalaal and had rivers and streams gliding beneath an endless shade of vine trees, palm trees, pomegranate trees, apple trees, quince trees, pear trees, apricot trees, peach trees, plum trees, jujube trees, mulberry trees, carob trees, banana trees, lemon trees, watermelon trees, cucumber trees, walnut trees, almond trees, pistachio trees, hazelnut trees, chestnut trees, coconut trees, oak trees, medlar trees and poppy trees; and all the paradisial trees had fine gold and silver trunks, and branches of emeralds, rubies and pearls.

13

The second paradise was Jannat Salaam, an open space of meadows, hills and vast horizons, with the refreshing water of the river Baidah meandering peacefully through the hills, the meadows and the vast horizons.

14

In the centre of Jannat Salaam stood the Zill Mamdood Tree whose shadow a rider would cross in a hundred years.

15

Under the shade of the Zill Mamdood Tree the paradisians routinely met and discussed paradisial affairs.

16

The third paradise was Jannat Adan and had the colourful mountain Jabal Toor, the river of ginger wine Zanjabeel and Wadi Afyah which was so wide that it had chains of muskscented dunes across.

17

Jannat Adan was the metropolis of the seven paradises, and on Fridays Allah descended on Wadi Afyah to meet the paradisians so they could talk to Him and make a wish.

18

The fourth paradise was Jannat Ma'wa and had the springs Ain Salsabeel and Ain Tasneem, and the river Harwal, and along the banks of Harwal were the singing trees whose wide ranging repertoire the paradisians loved to hear.

19

When the paradisians wanted to listen to the singing trees they said: "Let us go and listen to the singing trees of Harwal", and in no time the paradisians were sitting by the banks of Harwal and listening to the joyful songs of the singing trees.

20

The fifth paradise was Jannat Khuld and had the Khuld Tree whose leaves shaded an area a rider would cross in a hundred years.

21

In Jannat Khuld Allah sowed a pearl in a musk-camphor-ambergris-scented soil, and out of the pearl the scented Tooba Tree grew with yellow flowers and incredibly long and thick branches casting shadows the fastest horse would cross in a hundred years.

22

The trunk and the branches of the scented Tooba Tree produced pure honeysweet gum, and around the scented Tooba Tree were saffron grass and sandalwood burning without fuel.

23

The ruby buds of the scented Tooba Tree were daily plucked and opened by the paradisians to obtain readymade gold-threaded silk clothes in colourful prints, and if a leaf from the scented Tooba Tree fell on our earth, our earth would explode in a blaze of light.

24

Jannat Khuld had the rivers Raheeq and Ma'een bubbling out of the roots of the scented Tooba Tree.

25

The sixth paradise was Jannat Firdaws and had the river of invigoration Kawthar, which had a concave bed and banks of mother of pearl, running through extensive open plains, fertile wadis, vineyards and gardens.

26

The seventh paradise was Jannat Na'eem, a stretch of vineyards and palm groves.

27

Jannat Na'eem had four springs, one of honey, one of wine, one of milk and one of water, all bubbling out of the roots of the scented Tooba Tree.

28

The seven paradises, whose overall colour was white, had a fine muskscented white and gold and silver and saffron soil with pebbles of rubies and pearls.

29

The seven paradises were forever as bright as the hour before sunrise, and had no summer or winter, nor sun or moon, nor night or day, nor hot or cold weather, nor winds or clouds, and only the opening and closing of their gates indicated the passage of time.

30

Allah said to the seven paradises: “I have created you as the rewarding home for those who obey Me.”

31

The paradisians lived in tentlike homes of concave emeralds, rubies, corals and white and yellow gems in all shades, and all the rooms of the paradisial homes had gold doors and domed terraces overlooking the gardens and the garden walls of gold and silver bricks.

32

The paradisial homes had rooms with mirrors and gold and silver combs and ruby beds with silk coverings and pillows and mattresses stuffed with raw silk.

33

The paradisial homes had rooms with silk coverings and carpets and cushions and mattresses stuffed with raw silk.

34

The paradisial homes had rooms with gold and silver trays full of gold and silver incense burners, plates, jars, pitchers and cups, and glasses and bottles of finely cut glass.

35

In the courtyard of each paradisial home were a clothes tree and a jewellery tree whose buds contained the clothes and the jewellery the residents desired, and all the desired clothes were studded with corals and pearls.

36

When the paradisians wished to have company they plucked a fruit from the companion tree and opened it, and the desired companion sprang out of the fruit.

37

When the paradisians wished to be in the company of other paradisians, the responsive paradisians entered each other's face.

38

And if the paradisians wished to have a child, the child was conceived and delivered and was a fully grown youth in no time.

39

When the paradisians wished to have something, a wishing cloud passed over them raining down whatever they wished.

40

When the paradisians felt like getting paradisial scented flowers and fruit, they went to a paradisial tree and looked at a branch, and the branch bent down so the paradisians could reach the desired paradisial scented flowers and fruit.

41

And when the paradisians felt like growing their own plants, they sowed seeds in the paradisial fields and the seeds grew instantly into the desired plants.

42

The paradisians wandered around the seven paradises on winged ruby horses and winged gemwhite camels they plucked out of the buds of the travel trees in their gardens, and when they wished to be instantly in another location they thought of the wishing beam and they were beamed instantly to their desired destination.

43

And if the paradisians wanted to buy or sell whatever they wished, they went to the paradisial trade fairs held regularly in the seven paradises, and when they found the goods they desired the buyer and the seller concluded the deal by entering each other's face, and at the end of each paradisial trade fair the paradisians returned to their paradisial homes with radiant faces.

44

Outside Baab Tawba were two rivers: the river of radiance Baariq running under a great ruby dome, and the river of revivification Hayaat which had a bed of saffron and roses, and banks of gold studded with pearls.

45

Allah appointed Israafeel, who was the tallest and the strongest and had the most melodious voice of all the angels, angel of the Lawh and the Soor and His Messenger to the angels, Noor angel of light, the sunlight colour Rooh Jibreel angel of war and winds and earthquakes, Sama angel of the seven heavens, Atheer angel of the celestial regions, Ard angel of the seven earths, Maa angel of water, Jawhar angel of metals and precious stones, Durr angel of pearls, Dukhaan angel of smoke, Zabad angel of foam, Hawaa angel of air, Naseem angel of breeze, Nahr angel of rivers, Ghadeer angel of streams, Ain angel of springs, Tal angel of hills, Wadi angel of valleys, Sahl angel of plains, Barad angel of hailstones and snow, Sakhr angel of rocks, Hajar angel of stones, Raml angel of sand, Tarab angel of music, Teeb angel of perfume, Karm angel of wine, Ridwaan angel of the seven paradises, the green Mikaa'eel angel of rain and vegetation, Hayawaan angel of animals, Hoot angel of fish, Mawj angel of waves and Bahr angel of the seven heavenly seas and the seven earthly seas and the seven seas and the skysea, and when Bahr walked in the seven heavenly seas or in the seven earthly seas or in the seven seas or in the skysea there was high tide and low tide.

SURA SIX

The Creation of Hell, Haarith and the Genii

1

A thousand years after the creation of paradise Allah created hell from the Light of His Throne and divided hell into seven hells, and placed one hell above another hell, and linked one hell to another hell by an infernal razorsharp hairline arched bridge which took three thousand years to cross.

2

Each hell was hotter than the hell above it and had innumerable chambers, and each infernal chamber was considerably larger than the seven earths.

3

The seven hells were surrounded by four infernal walls of firebricks, and each infernal wall had a thickness of a distance of forty years.

4

The seven hells had seven gates, and each infernal gate, which was kept at a distance of over seventy years from the gate of the next hell and had an ironring knocker, consisted of two gate-leaves whose width spanned a distance of forty years, and was seventy times sturdier than the gate of the hell above it.

5

The seven infernal gates were named after their respective hells.

6

Allah closed the seven gates of the seven hells and lit the fires of the seven hells and let them burn for a thousand years until they were white, and let them burn again for a thousand years until they were red, and let them burn again for another thousand years until they were black as tar.

7

The seven hells said to Allah: "Lord, our fires will eat us up."

8

Allah said to the seven hells: "Have no fear. Your fires will not eat you up."

9

Allah made the seven hells breathe, and out of the seven hells' breath Allah created the infernal seasons: Winter and Summer.

10

In the Winter the seven hells breathed their frosty Winter Breath Zamhareer to cool the uncontrollable tempers of the infernal fires, and in the Summer the seven hells breathed their searing Summer Breath Samoom to whip up the uncontrollable tempers of the infernal fires, and through their Zamhareerian

Breath and their Samoomian Breath the seven hells regulated their infernal fires.

11

The first hell was Jahannam and had at its incredibly deep bottom Wadi Jub Hazan, Wadi Lamlam, Wadi Habhab, Wadi Ghai, Wadi Mawbiq, Wadi Athaam and Wadi Wail whose depth was a distance of forty autumns, and the Jahannam wadis were overlooked by Jabal Aqaba which took seven thousand years to climb.

12

The second hell was Hutama and had the prison Sijn Boolas whose roof was the searing shadows of the Boolasian fires of Naar Anyaar.

13

The third hell was Lada and had the wells Bi'r Mansa and Bi'r Falaq whose mouth was the size of a wadi.

14

The fourth hell was Sa'eer and had the infernals' bathing firelake Hawd Khabaal and the infernals' drinking firesprings: Ain Hameem whose Samoomian rusty firewater bubbled out like molten copper; and Ain Ghassaaq whose Zamhareerian greyish firewater bubbled out like liquid lead, and if a bucket of Ain Ghassaaq's Zamhareerian greyish firewater was spilt on our earth, the stench of the Zamhareerian greyish firewater would kill all earthly living creatures.

15

The fifth hell was Saqar and had the Zaqqoom Tree shaped like the heads of the Shayaateen, and its firefruit was the food of the infernals, and if a juicedrop of firefruit fell on the seas of our earth it would kill all sea life.

16

The sixth hell was Jaheem and had the mountain of fire Jabal Sa'ood, and those destined to climb Jabal Sa'ood would climb up to a distance of seventy autumns before tumbling down to the bottom to start climbing all over again.

17

When the climbers touched Jabal Sa'ood with their hands and feet the mountainfire melted their hands and feet, and when they lifted their hands and feet out of the mountainfire their hands and feet came to life again.

18

The seventh hell was Haawiya and was deeper than a distance of seventy years, and had the shade mountain of black smoke Jabal Yahmoom, and only the doomed were thrown down Haawiya.

19

When the doomed touched the bottom of Haawiya, the bottom of Haawiya moved slowly upwards until it levelled with the surface of Haawiya and dumped the doomed who were thrown again down Haawiya.

20

The seven hells were forever dark, their flames never stopped burning, and out of the castlesize, glowless sparks of hellfire Allah created Haarith and the genii and moved them to the seven paradises to worship Him together with the angels.

21

In the seven paradises and the seven heavens the angels, Haarith and the genii did not procreate.

22

Allah said to the seven hells: “I have created you as the punishment home for those who disobey Me.”

23

The angels were frightened by the fires of hell.

24

The angels said to Allah: “Lord, why have You created these fires and for whom have You created them?”

25

Allah said sternly: “I have created the fires of hell for those who disobey Me.”

26

The angels said: "Lord, we will never disobey You."

27

Some of the infernals had their hands firecuffed to their necks so they could be punished through their faces; and if a ring of one of the firecuffs was exposed to the mountains of our earth, the mountains of our earth would turn into black water.

28

Some of the infernals had their locks firechained backwards to their feet so they could be punished through their backs; and if a ring of one of the firechains was exposed to the mountains of our earth from a distance of five hundred years, the mountains of our earth would melt away.

29

Some of the infernals were pounded by redhot iron hammers as they went round redhot grinding stones dragging their entrails on grounds of fire.

30

Some of the infernals were firechained to firepegs, and whenever the seven hells belched, the infernals caught in the belching-up were hurled into a distance of five hundred years and pulled back the same day.

31

Some of the infernals were dragged by their grabbed faces along grounds of fire, and some were thrown in the fires of hell as fuel, and when their bodies got burnt, they were spewed out, and the burnt up bodies came to life to be thrown in the fires again.

32

Sometimes Allah let pitchblack clouds pass over the infernals and said: “What would you like?”

33

The infernals would remember the clouds of the earth and say: “Lord, give us a drink”, and the pitchblack clouds rained firecuffs, firechains and firestones on them.

34

The infernals wore fireclothes and every time their skin got burnt, their burnt-up skin came to life again.

35

The souls of the infernals were trapped in their throats of chokedscreams, and all the infernals were confined to their destined hells, and if an infernal was exposed to our earth the infernal's hellish stench and repulsive sight would kill all humans.

36

The seven paradises were separated from the seven hells by the Bain region, and along the Bain region were the infernal hairline road Siraat, the barrier hill of Aqaba, the seven seas, the barrier hill of A'raaf and the paradisial hairline road Siraat, and these obstacles stopped the infernals from getting to the seven paradises.

37

No infernals could ever escape from their destined hells, but if Allah willed to move infernals to the seven paradises He cued the angels to perform the transfer ritual.

38

The angels brought the infernals out of their destined hells like snapped sesame twigs and bathed them in Hayaat to revive them and cleanse them of all infernal traces, and the infernals came out of Hayaat revived and as clean as parchment sheets.

39

The angels bathed the revived and cleansed infernals in Baariq, and the revived and cleansed infernals came out of Baariq as paradisial radiant youths, and the angels then ushered the paradisial radiant youths to the seven paradises through Baab Tawba.

40

Allah appointed Naar angel of fire and the seven seas of fire, Zalaam angel of darkness, Bain angel of the Bain region, Jabal angel of mountains, Siraat angel of roads, Jisr angel of bridges, Aqaba angel of the barrier hill of Aqaba, A'raaf angel of the barrier hill of A'raaf, Hawd angel of lakes, Bi'r angel of wells, Haarith chief guard of the seven paradises, the genii guards of the seven paradises and Maalik angel of the seven hells with a team of eighteen Zabaaniya police angels to help him in his task, and the Zabaaniya police angels had lightning blue eyes and thornlike fangs and shoulders as wide as a distance of one year, and they had enormous hands, and with each hand they could grab and throw seventy thousand people to any place in the seven hells, and their mouths were belching furnaces.

SURA SEVEN

The Seven Heavens

1

In the first of the seven heavens, the burnished iron earthly heaven Birqi, Allah created the Naareeh angels out of fire and wind, and appointed Barq angel of lightning, and Ra'd angel of thunder and clouds and leader of the Naareeh angels.

2

Ra'd went about with his iron staff tending his clouds like a camelier shepherding his camels.

3

There was a tree in Jannat Jalaal whose black gargantuan fruit of rainwater was regularly picked by Mikaa'eel and deposited in Abzam in the earthly heaven Birqi, where the stationed clouds sucked the rainwater from the black gargantuan fruit, then sailed to predetermined destinations, where Ra'd thundered and Barq flashopened the seals of the clouds, and the clouds released their load of rainwater then sailed back to Abzam for their new assignment.

4

The second brass heaven Bina had a motley of angels with shoulders growing very long hair of immeasurable length.

5

Among the Bina angels was the angel of harmony Habeeb who was half fire and half ice clipped together in such a way neither the fire melted the ice nor the ice extinguished the fire.

6

When Allah willed snow to fall on a region He aired His Will to Habeeb, and Habeeb fluttered his wings and the snow flaked off his wings and fell on the region concerned.

7

The third pearlgrey heaven Saqf had angels standing in rows like huge castles with shoulders growing very long hair of immeasurable length.

8

Each Saqf angel had many faces, and some angels had two wings and others had three wings, four wings, five wings and six wings.

9

The fourth silver heaven Taraa'iq had myriads and myriads of angels, and only Allah knew how many they were, for in each successive heaven were twice as many angels as in the preceding heaven.

10

The Taraa'iq angels were so absorbed in their prayers that if one of them was away on a mission the angels next to him would be unaware of his absence.

11

The fifth gold heaven Tibaaq had more angels than all the angels in the first four heavens.

12

The sixth ruby heaven Aroos had the great army of myriads and myriads of Karoobi angels led by an angel who commanded seventy thousand angels, and each angel also commanded seventy thousand angels.

13

Allah assigned the Aroos angels to deal with earthly matters.

14

The seventh white pearl heaven Raqee had Allah's soldier angels led by an angel who commanded seven hundred thousand angels, and each angel commanded as many angels as the grains of dust and sand, pebbles, green leaves, raindrops and the angels in the seven heavens and the seven earths.

15

In the seventh heaven was Tasbeeh, an enormously tall angel in the shape of a white cockerel whose greenfeathered crest was beneath Allah's Throne and whose feet dug deep into the seventh heaven.

16

Tasbeeh had green down under his white feathers and one wing of snow was stretched eastwards, and one wing of fire was stretched westwards.

17

At dawn and dusk Tasbeeh called Allah's Creatures to prayer by flapping and clapping his wings of snow and fire, and neither the wing of snow extinguished the wing of fire nor the wing of fire melted the wing of snow.

18

When the cockerels of the earth heard Tasbeeh's wings flapping and clapping they flapped their wings and crowed, and stopped when Tasbeeh ceased flapping and clapping his wings.

19

In the seventh heaven Raqee Allah planted the Sidrat Muntaha Tree which had extensive pearl, ruby and emerald branches and giant leaves, and each giant leaf threw a shade that sheltered a hundred people, and on each giant leaf was an angel praying.

20

The Sidrat Muntaha Tree was the favourite haunt of the golden butterflies, and its shade spread all over the seventh heaven.

21

No earthlings nor heavenly angels could go beyond the Sidrat Muntaha Tree, but their cargoes would be transferred to the celestial terminal of the Sidrat Muntaha Tree to be collected by the celestial angels and transported to Allah.

22

The celestial cargoes were likewise transited to the heavenly terminal of the Sidrat Muntaha Tree to be collected by the earthlings and the heavenly angels concerned.

23

The seven heavens had seven windows and seven gates, and each heavenly gate consisted of two gateleaves.

24

The seven heavenly gates were named after their respective heavens.

25

Allah charged the angel Hamilsama to carry the seven heavens on his shoulders and rotate them like a grinding stone.

SURA EIGHT

The Throne of Allah

1

In the celestial region of Dukhaan which was at a distance of five hundred years above the seventh heaven Allah stationed His Own soldier angels who were the most powerful of all the angels except for Jibreel and the Throne Bearers among whom was Israafeel.

2

Each Throne Bearer had a multicoloured body with many faces and many wings, and none of the Throne Bearers resembled one another.

3

And if a Throne Bearer spread his wings the whole world would be wrapped in one of his feathers, and if a Throne Bearer opened his mouth he would swallow the seven heavens and the seven earths like the desert swallowing a grain of sand, and only Allah knew how many Throne Bearers there were.

4

Above the celestial region of Dukhaan was the Sea of Clouds which was as dense as the seven heavens and the seven earths and as distant from the seventh heaven as from the seventh heaven to the seventh earth.

5

Beyond the Sea of Clouds were the limitless Deserts of Light.

6

Beyond the Deserts of Light was the Masjoor Sea of still waters which had angels with firespears the length of a distance of one year, and the Masjoor Sea was guarded by the angel Masjoor, and only Allah knew how big Masjoor was, and if the seven heavens were put in the mouth of Masjoor the seven heavens would look like a mustard seed in the depth of the ocean, and if Masjoor appeared to the creatures of the seven heavens and the seven earths, the creatures would be burnt by his explosively blazing light.

7

Beyond the Masjoor Sea were four rivers: the River of Light, the River of Fire, the River of Ice and the River of Water.

8

Beyond the four rivers were four hundred and ninety Shields of alternating light, fire, darkness, smoke, clouds, lightnings and thunders, and each Shield was as long and as wide as a distance of five hundred years, and the Shields were guarded by the angel Haajib, and only Allah knew how big Haajib was.

9

And high above the Shields was Allah's home Illiyyeen.

10

Allah ordered the Throne Bearers: "Move My Throne to Illiyyeen."

11

The Throne Bearers tried to lift Allah's Throne off the water, but the weight of Allah's Throne was beyond their strength.

12

The Throne Bearers tried again and again to lift Allah's Throne off the water, but the weight of Allah's Throne was still beyond their strength.

13

Allah said to the Throne Bearers: "When you lift My Throne say 'With Allah's Will we lift Allah's Throne to Illiyyeen'."

14

The Throne Bearers held the feet of Allah's Throne with their hands and said: "With Allah's Will we lift Allah's Throne to Illiyyeen," and Allah's Throne became as light as a single hair in a strong body, and the Throne Bearers lifted Allah's Throne with ease to Illiyyeen, and Allah's Throne rested on the shoulders of the Throne Bearers who were so tall that their feet reached as far as a distance of five hundred years below the seventh earth, and each foot of the Throne Bearers stretched like a distance of seven thousand years.

15

Allah's Throne had hundreds of thousands of legs kept apart by a distance a fast flying bird would cross in eighty thousand years, and each leg had the density of the seven heavens and the seven earths.

16

No angel or creature could look at the megapower Light of Allah's Throne made of eighty thousand colours changed daily.

17

And if the whole of creation was placed on Allah's Throne it would look like a ring in the desert or like a lamp suspended between the seven heavens and the seven earths.

18

And if all the creatures of the seven paradises and the seven heavens and the seven earths went round Allah's Throne they would look like a droplet in the ocean.

19

Allah ringed His Throne with a protective, pearlheaded, goldbodied, rubyeyed serpent that had forty thousand wings, and on each wing, which spanned a distance of five hundred years, stood an angel with an extended, luminous spear in his hand saying his prayers; and only Allah knew how big the serpent was.

20

There was an angel by the name of Hazqyaa'eel who had eighteen thousand wings, and each wing was separated from the next wing by a distance of five hundred years.

21

Once Hazqyaa'eel said to himself: "I wonder what My Lord's Throne is like."

22

Allah read Hazqyaa'eel's thoughts.

23

Haarith appeared out of nowhere and said to Hazqyaa'eel: "Hazqyaa'eel, look at yourself. What a magnificent form you have. And with those powerful wings of yours, you must be the mightiest angel around. I bet there is not a place you cannot reach, not even Allah's Throne. I have often wondered what Allah's Throne is like, but since Allah's Throne is beyond me, I will never know because I dont have your powerful wings. Have you ever thought what Allah's Throne is like?"

24

Hazqyaa'eel said: "It crossed my mind, but I never gave it much thought."

25

Haarith said: “You should think about it. What is the point of having such powerful wings if you dont use them?”

26

Hazqyaa’eel said: “With my powerful wings, Haarith, no place is beyond me, not even Allah’s Throne.”

27

Haarith said: “What is stopping you? If I was you I would find out straight away what Allah’s Throne is like.”

28

Hazqyaa’eel thought: “Maybe I should find out what Allah’s Throne is like.”

29

Allah read Hazqyaa’eel’s thoughts.

30

Allah doubled Hazqyaa’eel’s eighteen thousand wings to thirty six thousand wings and said: “Hazqyaa’eel, fly to My Throne.”

31

Hazqyaa’eel flew for twenty thousand years, and still Hazqyaa’eel was nowhere near the feet of Allah’s Throne.

32

Allah doubled Hazqyaa'eel's thirty six thousand wings to seventy two thousand wings and said: "Hazqyaa'eel, fly to My Throne."

33

Hazqyaa'eel flew for thirty thousand years, and still Hazqyaa'eel was nowhere near the feet of Allah's Throne.

34

Allah said to Hazqyaa'eel: "Hazqyaa'eel, inspite of your strength and your powerful wings you will never reach the feet of My Throne, even if you fly from now until I order Israafeel to blow the Soor at the end of time."

35

Another angel by the name of Dardaa'eel who had sixteen thousand wings, and each wing was separated from the next wing by air which filled a distance of five hundred years, said to himself more than once: "Is there anything beyond My Lord and His Throne?"

36

Allah read Dardaa'eel's thoughts.

37

Haarith met Dardaa'eel and said: "Dardaa'eel, what do you do with those powerful powerful wings of yours? I wish I had your powerful powerful wings, and if I had them I would fly and fly and go beyond Allah's Throne, as it is the only place I havent yet explored. But that is wishful thinking. With my poor wings I doubt that I could make it even to the feet of Allah's Throne. Have you ever thought of going there?"

38

Dardaa'eel said: "I thought about it."

39

Haarith said: "You should do something about it."

40

Dardaa'eel said: "My powerful powerful wings, Haarith, can take me anywhere I like, even beyond Allah's Throne."

41

Haarith said: "Why not explore beyond Allah's Throne?"

42

Dardaa'eel thought: "Maybe I should explore beyond Allah's Throne."

43

Allah read Dardaa'eel's thoughts.

44

Allah doubled Dardaa'eel's sixteen thousand wings to thirty two thousand wings and said: "Dardaa'eel, fly to wherever you wish."

45

Dardaa'eel flew for five hundred years and his head was nowhere near the feet of Allah's Throne.

46

Allah said to Dardaa'eel: "Dardaa'eel, stop there. No matter how long you fly, you will never reach the feet of My Throne. My Throne is beyond you, and I am beyond My Throne, and there is nothing beyond Me. Go back to your place and stay put."

47

Dardaa'eel obeyed Allah's orders.

48

Allah's Throne thought: "I am the essence of Allah's creations. I am the noblest of All Creation."

49

Allah read His Throne's thoughts.

50

Allah encircled His Throne with a serpent that had seventy thousand wings, and each wing had seventy thousand feathers, and each feather had seventy thousand faces, and each face had seventy thousand mouths, and each mouth had seventy thousand tongues that never stopped praying.

51

Allah's Throne said to Allah, "Lord, what have I done?"

52

Allah said: "You have disobeyed Me."

53

Allah's Throne said: "Lord, I have not disobeyed You."

54

Allah said: "You have disobeyed Me in your thoughts."

55

Allah's Throne, now humbled, said: "Lord, if I have disobeyed You in my thoughts, forgive me."

56

Allah said to His humbled Throne: "You are forgiven."

SURA NINE

The Seven Earths

1

The first of the seven earths was our earth Adeem, and had the rivers Jaihaan, Saihaan, Tigres, Euphrates and Nile, which Jibreel brought on his wings from Jannat Jalaal.

2

The second earth Bisaat was the home of the Tams creatures who lived on their own flesh and drank their own blood, and in Bisaat Allah locked up the winds and guarded them with seventy thousand angels.

3

The third earth Thaqeela was the home of the Qais creatures who had human faces and human hands, but had doglike mouths, cattlelike legs, goatlike ears and sheeplike hair.

4

The Qais creatures wore no clothes, and their night coincided with our daytime and our night coincided with their daytime.

5

The fourth earth Bateeh was the home of the Jilla creatures who had wings but no eyes and no feet, and died only of old age.

6

The fourth earth Bateeh had sulphur rocks like mountains, which were used to stoke the fires of the seven hells.

7

The fifth earth Mihaad was the home of the Khashan creatures who lived on soil and their mothers' milk.

8

The fifth earth Mihaad had the scorpions of hell, that were as large as mules with spearlike tails one hundred and thirty five metres long, and each tail had three hundred and sixty poisonous spines, and each spine had three hundred and sixty poisonous cells, and each cell contained three hundred and sixty jars full of poison, and if one of the poison jars was exposed in the middle of our earth the smell of the poison would kill all creatures and vegetation.

9

The fifth earth Mihaad had also the serpents of hell, and each serpent was the length of a wadi and had eighteen thousand fangs, and each fang, like a tall palm tree, contained eighteen thousand jars full of poison, and if Allah ordered a serpent to strike a mountain with one of its fangs the mountain would be pulverised.

10

The sixth earth Sijjeen was the home of the Hathoom creatures who had black bodies and paws like wild beasts, and in Sijjeen Allah stored the crime files of the infernals.

11

The seventh earth Thara was the home of Iblees and his soldier Shayaateen and his dreaded weapons: the earthly frosty Zamhareerian Wind and the earthly searing Samoomian Wind, which Iblees developed out of his infernal breath.

12

The seven earths had seven windows and seven gates, and each earthly gate consisted of two gateleaves.

13

The seven earthly gates were named after their respective earths.

14

Allah charged the angel Hamilard to carry the seven earths on his shoulders, and Hamilard stretched his arms eastwards and westwards and held the foundations of the seven earths firmly with his hands.

15

Allah saw Hamilard's feet dangling and sent a paradisial bull called Rayyaan who had seventy thousand horns and forty thousand hooves so Hamilard could rest his feet on the hump of Rayyaan.

16

But Hamilard could not rest his feet on the hump of Rayyaan.

17

Allah sent a paradisial green stone whose density was like a distance of five hundred years and fixed it on the back of Rayyaan, between his hump and his ears, and Hamilard steadied himself on the paradisial green stone.

18

The horns of Rayyaan rose out of the seven earths heavenwards until their fine pointed tips formed a fence under the feet of Allah's Throne, and the nose of Rayyaan was under the sea, and when Rayyaan breathed there was high tide and low tide.

19

Allah assigned an angel to provide Rayyaan with his daily meals of a thousand trees from paradise, and each tree was as long as a day and a night.

20

Haarith pondered the mystery of Rayyaan's load and said to Rayyaan: "Rayyaan, what are you up to, carrying this incredibly heavy load? You will break your back if you go on like this."

21

Rayyaan said helplessly: "I am carrying the earth and its support. It is Allah's Will, Haarith."

22

Haarith teased: "You can still do something about easing your burden."

23

Rayyaan said with curiosity: "Like what?"

24

Haarith said casually: "Like throwing your load off your back, Allah or no Allah. If I was you I would not have anything on my back, even if it was Allah's Will. Be like me, the free and loadless Haarith."

25

Rayyaan said: "What shall I do?"

26

Haarith said: "Rayyaan, that paradisial green stone will leave a permanent scar on your back if you dont get rid of it."

27

Rayyaan said defensively: "I couldnt do that, Haarith."

28

Haarith said: "It is up to you."

29

Rayyaan weighed the merit of Haarith's advice and concluded: "There is sense in what Haarith said."

30

Rayyaan stretched his limbs, craned his neck and breathed deeply, and the paradisial green stone was easing gradually off his back.

31

Instantly Allah sent an insect the size of a butterfly called Aama flying through Rayyaan's nose.

32

Rayyaan could not breathe and screamed: "Lord, I cannot breathe, help me get rid of Aama."

33

Allah responded: "Rayyaan, you disobeyed Me."

34

Rayyaan said: "Lord, I did nothing of the kind."

35

Allah said: "You listened to Haarith's advice and disobeyed Me."

36

Rayyaan said: "Forgive me, Lord, I promise not to listen to Haarith again nor disobey You."

37

Allah said: "Rayyaan, you are forgiven."

38

Allah ordered Aama to leave Rayyaan's nose.

39

Aama flew out of Rayyaan's nose.

40

Rayyaan, relieved of his ordeal, prayed: "Labbaik, O Lord of All Creation."

41

But Rayyaan had nothing solid on which to rest his hooves.

42

Allah sent a green rock called Saikhoor, which was as big as the seven heavens and the seven earths, so Rayyaan could rest his hooves on Saikhoor.

43

Saikhoor had nine thousand holes, and in each hole was a sea, and only Allah knew how vast the sea was.

44

But there was nothing to sustain Saikhoor.

45

Allah sent an enormous fish called Noon from the first heavenly sea.

46

The eyes of Noon were so bright that no one could look at them.

47

The nostrils of Noon were so large that if all the seas of our earth were put in one of the nostrils they would look like a mustard seed in the desert.

48

Allah assigned an angel to provide Noon with his daily meals of a thousand fish from the still waters of the Masjoor Sea, and each fish was as long as a day and a night.

49

Allah piled enough sand to fill the seven heavens and the seven earths and ordered the seven winds to blow the sand onto the back of Noon to form a cushionmound on the back of Noon.

50

Allah loaded Saikhoor on the cushioned back of Noon, and Noon floated on the winds.

51

Haarith, amused by the way the earth had been propped up, said to Noon: "Noon, I have just been to see Rayyaan and he told me things that were not complimentary about you. He said you are not as strong as he is, and his skin is tougher than yours, and that is why your back is cushioned with a mound of soft sand so as to protect your delicate skin from the rough surface of Saikhoor."

52

Haarith's teasing words scratched the pride of Noon.

53

Noon said aggressively: “Haarith, tell Rayyaan that it is I who is stronger and has a tougher skin than his, because it is I who is carrying him and everything else with him, and to prove my point I will remove the sand mound off my back.”

54

Haarith said encouragingly: “Noon, if you only knew what you have on your back: angels, nations, animals, trees, rocks, sand and many other things. If you shake them off your cushioned back you will feel freer and much better.”

55

Noon said defensively: “I couldnt do that, Haarith.”

56

Haarith said: “Why not?”

57

Noon said: “It is Allah’s Will.”

58

Haarith said: “What has Allah got to do with it? You are the one who is carrying this useless load, not Allah. So it is up to you.”

59

Noon weighed the merit of Haarith's advice and concluded: "There is sense in what Haarith said."

60

As Noon was about to follow Haarith's advice, Allah sent Aama to plague Noon, and Aama landed between Noon's eyes and drilled through his brains.

61

Noon went wild and begged Allah: "Lord, what have I done? Lord, Aama is driving me mad, help me get rid of it."

62

Allah responded: "You thought of following Haarith's advice."

63

Noon said: "Lord, I did not follow Haarith's advice."

64

Allah said: "But you thought of disobeying Me."

65

Noon said: "Forgive me, Lord, I promise not to listen to Haarith again nor disobey You."

66

Allah said: “Noon, you are forgiven.”

67

Allah ordered Aama to leave Noon’s head.

68

Aama flew out of Noon’s head.

69

Noon, relieved of his ordeal, prayed: “Labbaik, O Lord of All Creation.”

70

The earth was rocking on the water like a ship on the waves.

71

The earth prayed: “Lord, I am shaking, it is the wind and the waves. Lord, help me steady myself otherwise everything will collapse.”

72

Allah said to the earth: “Earth, have no fear.”

73

Allah thought: “I have to steady the earth very quickly before the earth falls apart and messes up My Creation Plan.”

74

Allah pegged down the earth with the mountains He created out of the waves, and put a sea of fire under each earthly sea, and when Naar walked in the seas of fire volcanic lavae jetted out of the earth.

75

Around the earth Allah threw a veil of darkness.

76

Beyond the veil of darkness Allah created the great skygreen Qaaf mountain out of an emerald, and appointed Qaaf angel of the Qaaf mountain.

77

The Qaaf mountain whose peak touched the skyline had a head, a face, teeth and roots which formed a chain of small mountains connected to every region on earth so that when Allah willed to punish a region He aired His Will to Qaaf and Qaaf shook the root of the region concerned and triggered an earthquake.

78

Beyond the Qaaf mountain were thousands and thousands of earths which Allah created out of the same foam He used to create our earth.

79

Among these earths was the snowmountain earth whose length and breadth was a distance of five hundred years, and beyond the snowmountain earth was the icemountain earth whose length and breadth was a distance of five hundred years.

80

Beyond the icemountain earth were seventy thousand silver earths, and beyond the silver earths were seventy thousand iron earths, and beyond the iron earths were seventy thousand musk earths, and the length of each of these earths was a distance of ten thousand years, and the width of each of these earths was a distance of ten thousand years, and these earths, though bright, had no sun or moon, and were the homes of angels.

81

Beyond the musk earths were the Dark Seas, and beyond the Dark Seas was the Wind Shield, and beyond the Wind Shield was the white earth which was thirty times bigger than our earth, and on the white earth lived many nations, and beyond the white earth was a serpent encircling all the earths.

SURA TEN

The Creation of the Sun, the Moon, the Khunnas Planets, the Stars, Time and the Four Seasons

1

Allah created the sun and the moon from the Light of His Throne and transfixed them very far from the earth in case they floodlight the earth at all times and burn all earthly life and vetrify the rocks and the stones.

2

Allah ordered Jibreel to pass one of his wings three times over the moon's face to reduce the intensity of its light which was as bright as that of the sun.

3

Jibreel passed one of his wings three times over the moon's face and night and day were born and scars appeared on the moon's face.

4

Allah created the Khunnas planets from the Light of His Throne, and the Khunnas planets were Jupiter, Mars, Saturn, Mercury and Venus.

5

Allah located the Khunnas planets together with the sun and the moon in the seventh heavenly sea so each could rotate in its orbit.

6

Allah created the stars out of daylight and hung them in the sky like lanterns in a mosque, and made the Milky Way the gateway to the seven heavens.

7

Allah created time out of the movements of the sun, the moon, the Khunnas planets and the stars.

8

And out of time Allah created the four earthly seasons: Winter, Spring, Summer and Autumn.

9

Allah appointed Shams angel of the sun, Qamar angel of the moon, Mushtaree angel of Jupiter, Marreekh angel of Mars, Zuhal angel of Saturn, Utaarid angel of Mercury, Zahra angel of Venus, Majarra angel of the Milky Way, Sharaaheel angel of the night, Haraameel angel of the day, Kusoof angel of the eclipse, Qawsallah angel of the rainbow, Dahr angel of time, Shita angel of Winter, Rabee angel of Spring, Saif angel of Summer, Khareef angel of Autumn and a Najm angel for each star.

SURA ELEVEN

Night and Day and the Eclipse of the Sun and the Moon

1

Allah created two wheels from the Light of His Throne, and each wheel had three hundred and sixty handles with a Birqi angel attached to each handle.

2

Allah confined one wheel to the sun and the other wheel to the moon.

3

Allah made a hundred and eighty springs on the east side of the sky and another hundred and eighty springs on the west side of the sky, and each spring was of boiling black clay bubbling like a cauldron on the fire.

4

Just before dawn Shams removed the sun from its orbit and ferried it up to the seventh heaven to pray facing Allah's Throne, then ferried it down into one of the eastern springs.

5

At dawnbreak three hundred and sixty Birqi angels grabbed the sun, and as they gently lifted it out of the eastern spring and seated it on its wheel the dawnlight flashed out of the eastern springs.

6

Jibreel donned the sun with the glowing dress of the hours Allah created from the Light of His Throne to tell the hours of the day.

7

Another three hundred and sixty Birqi angels, each angel attached to a handle, took over and slowly started to roll the wheel until it reached the west, Jibreel then removed the glowing dress of the hours and the Birqi angels took the sun off the wheel and dropped it in one of the western springs.

8

Shams lifted the sun out of the western spring and ferried it up to the seventh heaven to pray facing Allah's Throne, then ferried it down to its orbit and left it there until the following dawn.

9

Just before the evening Qamar removed the moon from its orbit and ferried it up to the seventh heaven to pray facing Allah's Throne, then ferried it down into one of the eastern springs.

10

In the evening three hundred and sixty Birqi angels grabbed the moon, and as they gently lifted it out of the eastern spring and seated it on its wheel the evening light flashed out of the eastern springs.

11

Jibreel donned the moon with the lambent dress of the hours Allah created from the Light of His Throne to tell the hours of the night.

12

Another three hundred and sixty Birqi angels, each angel attached to a handle, took over and slowly started to roll the wheel until it reached the west, Jibreel then removed the lambent dress of the hours and the Birqi angels took the moon off the wheel and dropped it in one of the western springs.

13

Qamar lifted the moon out of the western spring and ferried it up to the seventh heaven to pray facing Allah's Throne, then ferried it down to its orbit and left it there until the following evening.

14

In the east of the sky Allah created the barrier of darkness out of the night and erected it on the seventh earthly sea, and the barrier of darkness spanned a distance of several earthly nights.

15

In the east of the sky Haraameel stood with a white bead in his hand, and in the west of the sky Sharaaheel stood with a black bead in his hand.

16

Just before the evening Haraameel hung his white bead in the eastern sky, and when Qamar and Sharaaheel saw the white bead hanging in the eastern sky they got on with their tasks.

17

Towards the evening Sharaaheel arrived at the barrier of darkness, scooped a handful of darkness and waited for the sun to set in the west.

18

While waiting, Sharaaheel let the handful of darkness slip slowly through his fingers until it overwhelmed the twilight, then spread his wings over the earth and the sky and covered them with darkness.

19

Sharaaheel hung his black bead in the western sky, then reached for the white bead in the eastern sky and stretched it westwards until it touched the black bead, and when Shams saw the stretched white bead touching the black bead he got on with his task.

20

Sharaaheel let go of the stretched white bead, and as the stretched white bead slowly rolled back to its place in the eastern sky Sharaaheel folded his wings, gathered with both hands the handful of darkness he let slip through his fingers and, with the same hand he used to scoop it, deposited it on the western side of the seventh earthly sea, and it was transferred back to the barrier of darkness in the east of the seventh earthly sea.

21

Sharaaheel removed his black bead from the western sky and held it in his hand, and Haraameel removed his white bead from the eastern sky and held it in his hand, and both angels stood at their posts until it was time for them to get on with their tasks.

22

When Allah was displeased with the earthlings He ordered Kusoof to cause an eclipse.

23

Kusoof let the sun and the moon fall off the wheels and sink in the still waves of the skysea, causing an eclipse of the sun and the moon, which filled the earthlings with fear.

24

Kusoof then dived in the still waves of the skysea to retrieve the sun and the moon, and as he gently raised the sun and the moon out of the still waves of the skysea and put them back on their wheels, the light slowly spread throughout the world, and the earthlings jumped for joy.

25

When Allah was pleased with the earthlings He sent them His Salaams with the rainbow.

SURA TWELVE

The Earthly Beings

1

Long before Haarith and the genii landed on earth, Allah populated the earth with beings He created out of fire and soil.

2

The earthly beings called Jaans were of flesh and blood and of towering height, and had wings and could fly wherever they liked, but the seven paradises and the seven heavens were beyond their wings.

3

The Jaans were fiercely independent, and their ambition extended as far as their wings could fly.

4

The Jaans cut rocks and built cities.

5

The Jaans challenged Allah's Authority over the earth, and plunged the earth into a series of volcanic wars threatening its structural stability.

6

The earth prayed: "Lord, if the Jaans go on with their wars, I will not be around for long. Lord, help me."

7

Allah said to the earth: "Have no fear. The Jaans will not bother you any more."

8

Allah called Jibreel: "Jibreel, lead My Raqee soldier angels and destroy the Jaans."

9

Armed with Divine Will and angelic zeal, Jibreel swooped down on the Jaans and exterminated them.

10

Allah supplanted the Jaans with new earthly beings He created out of fire, water and soil.

11

The new earthly beings were called Hinns, and had reddish-white blood and exceptionally large, translucent bodies.

12

The Hinns cut rocks and built cities.

13

The Hinns summered in the east and wintered in the west.

14

The Hinns had a fiery blood temper, and for a thousand years blazed the earth with wars which burnt the earthly creatures and their homes.

15

The earthly creatures prayed urgently: "Lord, the Hinns are blazing the earth with their fiery blood wars. Lord, the Hinns are burning us alive with their fiery blood wars. Lord, save the earth from the fiery blood wars of the Hinns so we can live without wars. Lord, protect us from the Hinns. Lord, save the earth."

16

Allah responded to the urgent prayers of the earthly creatures: "Have no fear. The Hinns will not bother you any more."

17

Allah thought: "If I dont contain the Hinns in time they will burn up My earth and interfere with the progress of My Creation Plan."

18

Allah said ominously to the Hinns: "It is time I put a stop to your fiery blood wars which are burning My earthly creatures and hampering the growth of life on My earth. Now what will you do if I appoint a Caliph to rule you as My Representative?"

19

The Hinns lasered back: "We will disobey him and kill him."

20

Allah was fuming: "You dare defy Me. It is I Who created you and it is I Who will destroy you."

21

Allah created new beings out of winds, clouds, lightnings and soil, and ordered the new beings: "Destroy the Hinns".

22

The new beings, called Binns, who were physically bigger than the Hinns, swooped down on the Hinns, and with their weapons of winds and clouds and lightnings flashed the Hinns out of the earth.

23

The Binns cut rocks and built cities, and dug wells and rivers and filled them with water from the springs and the seas, and made waterwheels and bridges, and used to dive through the seven earths, and the seven earths were within their sight.

24

The Binn population grew rapidly, and when the earth reached bursting point, the Binns waged wars on each other and killed their opponents by trapping them in their homes and starving them to death.

25

The Binns hunted recklessly the earthly birds and beasts.

26

The terrorstricken earthly birds and beasts got together, and one of the birds said: “The Binns are killing us to feed their senseless appetite. What are we going to do?”

27

One of the beasts said: “The Binns are too much for us. Only Allah can bale us out.”

28

The earthly birds and beasts agreed to pray urgently for help.

29

The earthly birds and beasts prayed urgently: “Lord, the Binns have been killing us nonstop for five hundred years, and if they go on killing us at this rate there will be none of us left. Lord, save us from the hungry Binns.”

30

Allah responded to the urgent prayers of the earthly birds and beasts: "Have no fear. The Binns will not bother you any more."

31

Allah said ominously to the Binns: "You have been killing My earthly birds and beasts since the day I created you and I said nothing. Now what will you do if I appoint a Caliph to rule you as My Representative?"

32

The Binns simply said: "We will disobey him and kill him."

33

Allah angrily called Jibreel: "Jibreel, destroy the Binns with the Kharooq Wind."

34

Armed with Divine Will and angelic zeal, Jibreel released the Kharooq Wind and said: "Kharooq Wind, it is Allah's Will you go to the first earth Adeem and destroy the Binns."

35

Armed with the will to please Allah, the icy Kharooq Wind swirled out of the second earth Bisaat and swept the first earth Adeem, tore up the Binns and consumed them.

36

Allah replaced the Binns with new beings He created out of soil, who were of flesh and bones and more perceptive than the Binns.

37

The new beings, called Rimms, cut rocks and built cities, and never stopped trying Allah's patience by challenging His Authority and senselessly killing the peaceful earthly creatures.

38

Allah gave the Rimms a last chance: "I have had enough from you. Now what will you do if I appoint a Caliph to rule you as My Representative?"

39

The Rimms said forcefully: "We will disobey him and kill him, and there is nothing You can do."

40

Allah brought new beings out of the seas of our earth and ordered them: "Destroy the Rimms."

41

The new sea beings, called Timms, who were physically much bigger and stronger and more ambitious than the Rimms, bounced hungrily on the Rimms and devoured them.

42

The Timms cut rocks and built cities and moved about the seven earths and the seven earthly seas, scorching the seven earths with endless wars, and revelling in the crimes that vexed Allah.

43

Allah thought: "I have to contain the Timms before they lay claim to the seven earths and the seven earthly seas and interfere with the progress of My Creation Plan."

44

Allah chose a Caliph from the Timms as His Representative to discipline the Timms, but the Timms killed Allah's Caliph.

45

Allah called Haarith and His Raqee soldier angels and bellowed: "Haarith, lead My Raqee soldier angels and exterminate the Timms."

46

Armed with the will to fight for Allah's cause, Haarith and the Raqee soldier angels headed towards the earth and executed Allah's orders, and not a single Timm was spared.

47

On his way to paradise Haarith said presumptuously to himself: "I am the General of Allah's Raqee soldier angels. I am more noble than the angels."

48

Allah read Haarith's thoughts.

SURA THIRTEEN

The Expulsion of Haarith and the Genii

1

Haarith and the genii guarded the seven paradises for forty thousand years.

2

Haarith and the genii grew restless with their life of obedience and prayer.

3

Haarith and the genii lusted for power and fought one another, straining the calm of the seven paradises.

4

The angels who craved for peace and quiet so they could pray undisturbed invariably reminded Haarith and the genii: "Allah created us to worship Him."

5

Haarith and the genii argued animatedly: "It is true Allah created us to worship Him, but Allah must have had other reasons for creating us. We intend to find out."

6

Ridwaan said to Haarith and the genii: "You should be praying instead of provoking Allah. Allah will punish you for questioning His Will."

7

Haarith said: "We have been doing nothing but praying since we were created. Doesnt Allah get tired of listening to His Name being prayed up night and day? It seems pointless that Allah should have gone through all the trouble of creating us just to worship Him. Wherever we go we hear nothing but the babbling praises of Allah's Name. Allah certainly loves His Name, but is that the limit of His Imagination?"

8

Ridwaan said: "You had better start praying before you anger Allah."

9

Haarith said: "Why should we pray when praying numbs our will to be ourselves? If we stop praying Allah will lose His Grip on us, and if we join forces we can overthrow Him and seize His Throne."

10

Ridwaan said: "How do you propose to do that?"

11

Haarith said: “A coup.”

12

The angels were perturbed by the uncontrollable ambitions of Haarith and the genii and appealed to Allah to save the seven paradises from the troublesome Haarith and the genii.

13

Allah, alarmed by Haarith and the genii’s lust for power, thought: “I must act fast and preempt the genii’s intended coup. I must instil fear in the hearts and minds of My creatures.”

14

Allah scanned the angels whose presence scaped the seven paradises and the seven heavens and said: “Remember the fires of hell. Those who obey Me will be spared the punishment of the fires of hell.”

15

The angels said: “Lord, we will never disobey You.”

16

Allah then called Jibreel: “Jibreel, get Haarith and the genii out of My Sight and out of My paradise and as far away as possible from here.”

17

Armed with Divine Will and angelic zeal, Jibreel chased Haarith and the genii out of the seven paradises and scattered them on earth, in deserts and on islands, where, like all new arrivals, Haarith and the genii ceased to be immortal and acquired the earthly power of procreation.

SURA FOURTEEN

Powerstruggle

1

When Haarith and the genii landed on earth Allah warned them: "Do not kill My earthly creatures, nor engage in wars, for the shedding of blood is an unforgivable crime."

2

The genii settled down, then went about exploring the earth, and they could not resist hunting Allah's earthly creatures, and their lust for power engulfed them in wars, threatening Allah's hold on them.

3

Allah was patient.

4

The genii's defiance shocked Haarith who prudently broke away from them and withdrew to Wadi Abqar and devoted his time to prayer, and the name of Allah never parted his lips.

5

Haarith prayed for a thousand years.

6

In the end Haarith could not bear the clamour of the warring genii and the cries of the dying genii and earthly creatures, and implored Allah: “Lord, can I go back to paradise to worship You in peace?”

7

Allah raised Haarith to paradise and said: “As a reward for your piety and devotion to Me, I elevate you to the angelic position of guardian of the earthly heaven Birqi, and appoint you Caliph of the earth, and name you Azaazeel to stress your nobility and Divine-inspired strength.

8

Azaazeel prayed: “Thank you, O Lord of Wisdom, the Allseeing, the Allknowing, the Allpowerful, Our One and Only worshipped Lord, Lord of the Worlds, Lord of All Creation.”

9

Azaazeel construed from his noble title and position as guardian of the earthly heaven Birqi and Caliph of the earth and his reinforced Divine-inspired strength, which boosted his morale immensely: “I must have qualities the angels lack to be offered an angelic post.”

10

Allah read Azaazeel’s thoughts.

11

The wars of the genii dragged on for two thousand years.

12

The earthly creatures caught in the wars of the genii prayed for help: "Lord, since the appearance of the earthly beings and the landing of the genii on earth we have had nothing but wars. Is there no end to wars? Lord, the genii are destroying our habitat and hunting us to extinction. Lord, protect us from the genii. Lord, save Your earth."

13

Allah responded to the prayers of the earthly creatures: "Have no fear. The genii will not bother you any more."

14

Allah said ominously to the genii: "War, war, war. Is there anything else you can do other than waging wars and killing My earthly creatures I warned you not to harm? It is time you stopped warring on each other and killing My earthly creatures. Now what will you do if I appoint a Caliph to rule you as My Representative?"

15

The genii snapped: "We will disobey him and kill him. This is our earth and not Your paradise. What goes on our earth is not Your concern. You have no place on our earth. Stay out of our earth."

16

Allah, outraged by the genii's defiance, bellowed: "Azaazeel, lead My Raqee soldier angels and exterminate the genii."

17

Armed with the will to fight for Allah's cause, Azaazeel and the Raqee soldier angels headed for the earth and exterminated most of the genii and those who escaped were tracked down and banished to the sea, remote islands, deserts and the atmosphere.

18

Azaazeel returned to his earthly heaven Birqi pleased with himself: "I have done a great deed which no other angel or genie has done before."

19

Allah read Azaazeel's thoughts.

20

Allah created new earthly beings out of soil and placed them in the central region of the earth.

21

The new earthly beings called Nisnaases were of flesh and blood and exceptionally tall, and had no wings, and some of them had one eye, one arm and one leg, and others resembled monkeys.

22

The Nisnaases were fiercely independent, and had a piercing mind, and the way they coped with life on earth paralleled that of their human successors.

23

The Nisnaases were the last earthly beings Allah created before Adam and Hawwa.

SURA FIFTEEN

Allah's House Duraah

1

Seven thousand years after the genii's incident on earth Allah ordered the angels to meet Him in the seven heavens.

2

The angels thronged to meet Allah in the seven heavens.

3

Allah ordered Sama to open the windows of the seven heavens facing the earth.

4

Allah said to the angels: "Now let us see what the genii and the Nisnaases are up to."

5

The angels were stunned by the seismic scale of the genii's war, and the Nisnaases fighting for the control of the earth and no longer worshipping Allah.

6

The angels said to Allah: “Lord, the genii and the Nisnaases are Your creatures, and You sustain them, yet they are disobeying You.”

7

Allah said: “Not for long. I am going to create a new Man creature who will be My Caliph on earth, and through him I will sort out the genii and banish the Nisnaases from the earth.”

8

The angels said: “Lord, this new Man creature, like those before him, will disobey You and indulge in bloodshed, which is an unforgivable crime. Lord, we have never disobeyed You. Lord, if You appoint one of us as Your Caliph on earth, we will never disobey You.”

9

Allah said: “I know what you dont know. I will create the new Man creature out of earthly soil with My Own Hands, and through him I will control the earth.”

10

The angels deduced from Allah’s sharp response He was displeased with them.

11

The angels were frightened and sought refuge in the Shadow of Allah's Throne that spread all over the seven heavens and the seven paradises.

12

The angels appeased Allah's displeasure by saying their prayers while doing the Tawaaf round the Shadow of Allah's Throne.

13

After the distressed angels had prayed and done the Tawaaf round the Shadow of Allah's Throne for seven years Allah felt sorry for them.

14

Allah built a House on four pillars of emeralds in the earthly heaven Birqi, and topped it with a ruby and called it Duraah, and appointed Razeen angel of Duraah.

15

Allah said to the angels: "You dont have to pray while doing the Tawaaf round the Shadow of My Throne, you can now pray while doing the Tawaaf round My House Duraah."

16

The angels prayed and did the Tawaaf round Duraah with greater zeal than before: "Labbaik, O Lord, Labbaik. Labbaik, O Merciful Lord of Forgiveness and Love. Labbaik, O

Magnanimous Lord of Patience and Hope. Labbaik, O Lord of Wisdom, the Allseeing, the Allknowing. Labbaik, Our One and Only worshipped Lord, Lord of the Worlds, Lord of All Creation."

SURA SIXTEEN

The Statue of Man

1

Allah told the earth: “Earth, out of your soil I will create new Man creatures, some of whom will obey Me and others will disobey Me. Those who obey Me will go to paradise, but those who disobey Me will go to hell.”

2

The earth said: “Lord, could all the new Man creatures You will create out of my soil go to paradise?”

3

Allah said: “Only if they all obey Me.”

4

The thought that some of the new Man creatures Allah would create out of her soil would end up in hell so upset the earth that she wept and wept until her face was a landscape of tearful springs.

5

Allah called Jibreel: “Jibreel, go down to earth and get Me a handful of soil.”

6

Jibreel went down to earth and as he was about to scoop a handful of soil the earth said: "May Allah protect me if you reduce me in size and disfigure me and let part of me end up in hell."

7

Jibreel was moved by the earth's invocation of Allah's protection and returned to Allah without the soil and said: "Lord, I havent brought You any soil because the earth invoked Your protection and I couldnt get myself to reduce her in size and disfigure her and let part of her end up in hell."

8

Allah called Mikaa'eel: "Mikaa'eel, go down to earth and get Me a handful of soil."

9

Mikaa'eel went down to earth and, like Jibreel, was disarmed by the earth's invocation of Allah's protection and returned to Allah emptyhanded.

10

Allah called Azraa'eel: "Azraa'eel, go down to earth and get Me a handful of soil."

11

Azraa'eel went down to earth and as he was about to scoop a handful of soil the earth said: "May Allah protect me if you reduce me in size and disfigure me and let part of me end up in hell."

12

Azraa'eel, indifferent to the earth's invocation of Allah's protection, threw back coldly: "May Allah protect me if I disobey His orders," and scooped a handful of black, red and white soil from the mountains, the wadis and the plains of the four corners of the earth, and returned to Allah.

13

Azraa'eel said to Allah: "Lord, here is the handful of soil You asked for."

14

The earth cried and prayed: "Lord, Azraa'eel snatched a handful of soil from me, and was indifferent to my invocation of Your protection. Lord, tell Azraa'eel to give me back what he coldly snatched from me. Lord, help me get my soil back."

15

Allah said to the earth: "Calm down, it was I Who ordered Azraa'eel to get a handful of your soil. But have no fear, you will have back what was taken from you."

16

Allah said to Azraa'eel: "Azraa'eel, why were you indifferent to the earth when the earth invoked My protection?"

17

Azraa'eel said: "Lord, the desire to obey Your orders and the fear of displeasing You urged me to fulfil Your orders."

18

Allah said: "In that case, Azraa'eel, I appoint you as the angel of death."

19

All at once Azraa'eel's body was studded with the eyes of all living creatures, and when a living creature died, the eyes of the dead creature lost their glow and fell off Azraa'eel's body and the eyes of a newborn creature appeared in their place.

20

Jibreel soaked the threecolour soil in the deliciously fresh spring water of Ain Tasneem and kneaded it and left it for forty years until it stank and turned into mouldable clay, and out of the mouldable clay Allah shaped the Statue of Man in His Own Image with His Own Hands.

21

Allah let the cloud of worry and grief pass over the Statue of Man and release its load of worry and grief over it for forty years.

22

Allah let the cloud of joy pass over the Statue of Man and release its load of joy over it for a year.

23

Allah left the Statue of Man to dry and harden for forty years and then exhibited it for another forty years on the road through which the angels travelled up and down the heavens.

24

The angels marvelled at the beauty of the face and at the height of the Statue of Man as they had not seen anything like it before, not even on Allah's Throne that had pictures of all His creations.

25

The unique and imposing figure of the Statue of Man became the talk of the seven paradises and of the seven heavens.

26

The angels who had never seen Allah reflected: "This new Man creature is of stinking earthly soil and we are of Divine Light, and since we were created before all other creatures, we are superior to them as well as to this new Man creature. Let Allah create whatever He likes, but He will never create creatures more noble and more perceptive than us."

27

Allah read the angels' thoughts.

SURA SEVENTEEN

Azaazeel and the Statue of Man

1

Azaazeel was apprehensive about the Statue of Man, and whenever he saw it he slapped it and kicked it and a tinkling sound rang throughout its hollow form.

2

Sometimes Azaazeel slithered in through the Statue's mouth and explored its hollow form before slithering out of its bottom; and sometimes he slithered in through its bottom and slithered out of its mouth and said to the angels: "Dont be afraid of this strange creature of stinking earthly soil. He is hollow and brittle and will not last. What will you do if Allah appoints him as your commander?"

3

The angels replied: "We will obey Our Lord."

4

Azaazeel was intrigued by the Statue and said to it: "You were not created for the sake of your potterish sound but for some other reason."

5

Azaazeel then said to himself: “If Allah appoints this creature as my commander I will disobey him, and if Allah appoints me as his commander I will destroy him.”

6

Azaazeel pondered the hollow form of the Statue and concluded: “As this creature is hollow he will need food and drink.”

7

Allah read Azaazeel’s thoughts.

SURA EIGHTEEN

The Expulsion of Iblees

1

Allah summoned the angels and Azaazeel to the Statue of Man, and told them: “I have created the Statue of Man out of earthly soil in My Own Image with My Own Hands. Bow to the Statue of Man who is in My Own Image.”

2

The angels said to themselves: “We thought we were dearer to Allah than this creature of stinking earthly soil, because we are closer to Allah than all other creatures, and we never thought Allah would go so far as to order us to bow to an inferior creature.”

3

Allah read the angels’ thoughts.

4

The angels bowed to the Statue of Man but not Azaazeel.

5

The angels raised their heads and when they saw Azaazeel standing erect and looking scornfully at them they quickly bowed their heads again.

6

Allah said to Azaazeel: "Azaazeel, what is stopping you from bowing to the Statue of Man I created in My Own Image with My Own Hands?"

7

Azaazeel said: "Lord, so this is what You look like! Lord, what prompted You to create the Statue of Man in Your Own Image? Is it because You miss looking at Yourself? Or is it because You miss the company of other Allahs?"

8

Allah said: "There are no other Allahs, nor will there ever be. I am the One and Only Allah. I am Whole and Perfect. I miss nothing."

9

Azaazeel said: "Lord, do You want me to worship the Statue of Man who looks like You?"

10

Allah said: "No one is worshipped but Me. I am the One and Only worshipped Allah."

11

Azaazeel said: "Lord, why then is the Statue of Man in Your Own Image?"

12

Allah said: "You have not been summoned to question Me, but to obey My Will. Bow to the Statue of Man."

13

Azaazeel said: "Lord, are You aware of what You have done? By creating the Statue of Man in Your Own Image You have given him the illusion that he is a copy of You. Lord, do You want me to endorse such an illusion?"

14

Allah said: "It is My Will you bow to the Statue of Man."

15

Azaazeel said: "Lord, bowing is a form of praying. Lord, do You want me to pray to the Statue of Man and endorse his divine status? Lord, as the Statue of Man is a copy of You he will be just as curious as You are. Lord, I appeal to You to think again before You slip down this precipitous curiosity."

16

Allah said: "I know what I am doing. Just bow to the Statue of Man."

17

Azaazeel said: "Lord, I will bow only to You, and not to a copy of You."

18

Azaazeel's argument not to bow to the Statue of Man put Allah in a reflective mood.

19

Allah thought of Azaazeel's refusal to bow to the Statue of Man as a sign of Azaazeel's devotion.

20

Azaazeel perceived he was getting through to Allah.

21

To drill his unbowing point further Azaazeel said: "Lord, has the Statue of Man become Your equal?"

22

Allah said: "I have no equal."

23

Azaazeel said: "Lord, You expect me to bow to a creature I am superior to? I am older and stronger than this creature. You created me from fire and You created him from stinking earthly soil, and fire is more noble than earthly soil. You have endowed me with feathers and light and the crown of nobility. I was the chief guard of Your paradise. I am Your Caliph on earth and the General of Your Raqee soldier angels. I am the guardian of Your earthly heaven Birqi. I have worshipped You in paradise and on earth. I have...."

24

Allah cut in: "Azaazeel! You dare question My Will?"

25

Azaazeel said: "Lord, I am not questioning Your Will, but if You spare me the indignity of bowing to Your new creature of stinking earthly soil, I will worship You more fervently than the angels and with far greater zeal than before."

26

Allah said: "You will worship Me in the way I want, and not in the way you want!"

27

Azaazeel said: "Dont be angry with me, Lord. I can explain everything if You give me a chance, O Magnanimous Lord of Patience and Hope."

28

Allah said: "What is there to explain? You had your chance like the rest of the angels."

29

Azaazeel said: "But I am not an angel. I am Your Azaazeel."

30

Allah said: "Then bow."

31

Azaazeel said: "Lord, how can Your Azaazeel bow to this lowly creature?"

32

Allah said: "I am Your Lord and Creator, and you do as I say. Bow."

33

Azaazeel said: "Lord, I have a will of my own. Lord, You can take away my life but not my will."

34

Allah said: "There is no other will but My Will. Bow."

35

Azaazeel said: "Lord, by forcing me and the angels to bow to this creature of stinking earthly soil You are dislocating Your hierarchical structure that sustains Your Worlds. If You think Your original hierarchical structure was misconceived straightening it up now will topsyturvy it again."

36

Allah said: "Everything I do is well conceived. For the last time, bow."

37

Azaazeel said: "Why should I?"

38

Allah said: "Because I say so."

39

Azaazeel said: "Make me."

40

Allah said: "Bow! Bow! Bow!"

41

Azaazeel said: "Slow down, Lord. No need to be snappy over nothing, O Lord of Patience and Hope."

42

Allah said: "You will bow! You will bow! You will bow!"

43

Azaazeel grinned.

44

Allah blasted: "You are dismissed from your angelic position as guardian of My earthly heaven Birqi, and you are no longer My Caliph on earth nor the General of My Raqee soldier angels, and you are banned from My paradise. From now on you will be called Iblees, so you will never forget what you have lost."

45

Iblees was lost for words: "But Lord ... This is drastic Lord ... What I meant Lord ... Please Lord...."

46

"Jibreel! Throw this Iblees of despair and gloom out of My paradise! Now," Allah screamed His orders at Jibreel.

47

Allah's screaming orders fearstung the bowing angels, and each of the bowing angels said to himself: "Thank Allah, it is Iblees and not me."

48

Armed with Divine Will and angelic zeal, Jibreel pounced on Iblees, but Iblees eluded Jibreel's blow and escaped to the Masjoor Sea.

49

But the sanctuary Iblees sought became his temporary prison, for the Masjoor Sea angels apprehended him and ringed him with their firespears and reported him to Jibreel.

50

Jibreel caught up with Iblees and, together with the Masjoor Sea angels, chased him with stinging firespears out of the celestial region of Dukhaan and out of the seven heavens and down to the Euphrates in the first earth Adeem where Iblees disappeared out of the sight of the pursuing angels.

51

The boldness of Iblees and the events that followed caused a commotion in the seven heavens which confused the paradisial and heavenly angels, and only the return of Jibreel and the Masjoor Sea angels allayed the apprehensions of the paradisial and heavenly angels who were assured that Iblees was out of the way and all was well.

SURA NINETEEN

The Creation of Adam

1

Allah created the Soul of Man from His Own Breath four thousand years before Adam.

2

The Soul of Man was different from the souls of the angels and of all other creatures because the Soul of Man was bathed in paradisial and heavenly lights.

3

When Allah decided to breathe life into the Statue of Man He ordered the Soul: "Get inside the Statue of Man who is in My Own Image."

4

But the Soul refused to go inside the Statue and said: "Lord, the mouth of the Statue of Man is deep and dark."

5

Allah repeated the same order a second time and a third time, but the Soul refused again and again to go inside the Statue.

6

The fourth time Allah just said: "You will get inside the Statue of Man whether you like it or not, and you will leave the Statue of Man whether you like it or not."

7

The Soul entered the Statue through its mouth and went to its brains and stayed for two thousand years, then slid downwards to its eyes, and when it reached its nose the Statue sneezed, and the Soul tumbled down to the mouth, the tongue, the chest and the ribs, and when it reached the Statue's bellybutton the Statue looked at itself admiringly and said: "What a beautiful sight," and then the Statue felt hungry and tried to move but could not move.

8

Allah observed: "How impatient is this selfcentred creature."

9

The Soul took another five hundred years to reach every part of the Statue, and the Statue became a living body with flesh and bones, blood, veins and muscles.

10

Allah covered the flesh of the living body with a translucent ungual membrane which grew more radiant every day.

11

Allah called the new Man creature Adam after the first earth Adeem.

12

Jibreel said to Adam: “Adam, you are the first Man Allah has created in His Own Image with His Own Hands. Say thank you to Allah, Lord of All Creation, Who, in His Wisdom, created you out of earthly soil in His Own Image with His Own Hands.”

13

Adam said: “Thank You, O Lord of Wisdom, Lord of All Creation.”

SURA TWENTY

Wadi Afyah

1

Allah adorned Adam with paradisial attire through which his body glowed like sunlight and seated him on a couch and ordered the angels: "Carry Adam on your shoulders and show him around the seven paradises and the seven heavens."

2

The angels, who travelled at the speed of fifty thousand years a day, were excited to be in the company of Allah's lookalike Adam as they showed him around the seven paradises and the seven heavens for a hundred years.

3

At the end of Adam's tour of the seven paradises and the seven heavens Allah said to Jibreel: "Go to Ridwan and tell him to give you Maimoon, the mare I created for Adam."

4

Jibreel darted to Ridwaan and said: "Salaam, Ridwaan, I have come to collect Maimoon."

5

Ridwaan called Maimoon, and Maimoon, whom Allah had created out of musk with wings of gems and pearls and hooves of precious stones five hundred years before Adam, galloped gracefully to Ridwaan.

6

Ridwaan said to Maimoon: "Maimoon, Jibreel has come to collect you."

7

Jibreel returned to Allah with Maimoon.

8

Allah ordered Jibreel, Mikaa'eel and Israafeel: "Show Adam around the seven paradises."

9

Adam gazed admiringly at the gracefulness of Maimoon, and at the emerald and topaz saddle and the ruby bridles, then mounted and rode Maimoon flanked by Mikaa'eel on his right and Israafeel on his left and with Jibreel holding the bridles, and the three angels showed Adam around the seven paradises.

10

At the end of Adam's tour of the seven paradises, Allah ordered Jibreel: "Tell Adam and the angels to meet Me on Friday in Wadi Afyah."

11

Jibreel informed Adam and the angels of Allah's Will.

12

On Friday Adam and twenty thousand lines of angels waited for Allah in Wadi Afyah.

13

Allah descended on Wadi Afyah and greeted Adam, the angels and the paradisial creatures: "Salaam from Your Merciful and Loving Lord."

14

Adam, the angels and the paradisial creatures greeted Allah: "Salaam from Your obedient creatures, O Merciful and Loving Lord of the Worlds, Lord of All Creation."

15

Allah said to the angels: "Give the names of all the creatures and the plants in paradise."

16

The angels stood there perplexed, unable to give the names of all the creatures and the plants in paradise.

17

Allah said to the angels: “You say if I appoint Adam as My Caliph on earth he will disobey Me, but if I appoint one of you as My Caliph on earth you will never disobey Me.”

18

The angels said: “Yes, O Lord of All Creation.”

19

Allah said: “How can I appoint one of you as My Caliph on earth when you have failed to give the names of all the creatures and the plants in paradise. If you are unable to pinpoint what you see before you, how can you perceive what you cannot see.”

20

The angels said: “Lord, You know what we dont know.”

21

Allah said to Adam: “Adam, get on the minbar and give the names of all the creatures and the plants in paradise.”

22

Allah revealed the names of all the creatures and the plants in paradise to Adam.

23

With a luminous stick in his hand Adam scaled the seven steps of the minbar especially prepared for him, faced the angels and gave the names of all the creatures and the plants in paradise.

24

The angels were impressed by Adam's performance and acknowledged Adam's superior intelligence.

25

Allah said to the angels: "Now you see why I created Adam to be My Caliph on earth."

26

The angels said: "We only know what You taught us, O Lord of Wisdom, the Allseeing, the Allknowing."

27

Allah said: "I know the secrets of all of My Creations, and what goes through your minds."

28

Allah then said to Jibreel: "Give Adam a bunch of white grapes."

29

Jibreel picked a bunch of white grapes from the nearest vine tree and gave it to Adam and said: "Before you eat or do anything always say: 'By the Blessing of Allah, the Merciful Lord of Forgiveness and Love'."

30

Adam said: "By the Blessing of Allah, the Merciful Lord of Forgiveness and Love," then ate the bunch of white grapes, and that was the first bite Adam had since his creation.

SURA TWENTY ONE

The Creation of Hawwa

1

Allah watched Adam wandering on his own in the seven paradises for one year.

2

Allah thought: "Adam could do with a companion."

3

Allah cast a veil of sleep over Adam, and Adam dreamt of Allah removing one of his leftside ribs and creating out of that rib a creature that looked like him, in flesh and dress.

4

Adam awoke and was thrilled to find the creature he saw in his dream sitting beside him.

5

Adam said to the creature: "Who are you?"

6

The creature, who was as tall as Adam but had a finer skin and a softer voice, said: "One of Allah's creatures."

7

Adam said: "Why are you here?"

8

The creature said: "To keep each other's company."

9

Adam said to Allah: "Lord, who is this creature sitting beside me and who looks like me?"

10

Allah said: "This creature is a woman called Hawwa whom I created out of your rib in My Own Image with My Own Hands to be your companion. Since Hawwa was created out of you, she is as knowledgeable as you are."

11

The angels came to Adam and said, pointing at Hawwa: "Who is this creature who looks like you?"

12

Adam said: "A woman."

13

The angels said: "Why is this creature called woman?"

14
Adam said: “Because she was created out of Man.”

15
The angels said: “What is her name?”

16
Adam said: “Hawwa.”

17
The angels said: “Why is she called Hawwa?”

18
Adam said: “Because she was created out of a living knowledge.”

19
The angels said: “Why did Allah create her?”

20
Adam said: “So we could keep each other’s company.”

21
The angels brought chairs of precious stones for Adam and Hawwa.

22

Adam and Hawwa sat on the chairs, and the angels gathered around them.

23

Allah cued Jibreel to ask Him for Hawwa's hand in marriage on behalf of Adam.

24

Jibreel asked Allah for Hawwa's hand in marriage on behalf of Adam, and Allah, who acted as Hawwa's ward, consented.

25

Allah ordered Ridwaan to put up the wedding decorations throughout the seven paradises.

26

Ridwaan got on with the wedding decorations, and Allah and Jibreel performed the marriage ceremony with the angels as witnesses.

27

Then the angels showered Adam and Hawwa with confetti of paradisial flower petals.

SURA TWENTY TWO

The Testing Tree

1

Allah thought: "It is time Adam and Hawwa had companions."

2

Allah ordered a cloud to pass over His Throne and let its load of raindrops fall on His Throne.

3

The cloud sailed over Allah's Throne and let its load of raindrops fall on Allah's Throne, and when the raindrops touched Allah's Throne, a Houri and a Walad Mukhallad leapt out of each raindrop.

4

The skin of the Houris and of the Wuldaan Mukhalladoon was as fine and as transparent as the skin of an egg, and had the colour of a newly found pearl untouched by human hands, and if the wrist or the face or a single hair of a Houri or of a Walad Mukhallad was exposed to the seven heavens and the seven earths, the seven heavens and the seven earths would explode in a blaze of light.

5

Allah moved the Houris and the Wuldaan Mukhalladoon to the seven paradises and housed them in tentlike homes along the paradisial river banks so Adam and Hawwa could have company throughout the seven paradises.

6

Allah said to Adam and Hawwa: "I have created the Houris and the Wuldaan Mukhalladoon so you can have company anywhere in the seven paradises whenever you like."

7

Adam and Hawwa were happy to be in paradise and in the company of the Houris and the Wuldaan Mukhalladoon.

8

Allah faced Adam and Hawwa and said: "I have created paradise for those who obey Me. If you promise Me you will be obedient I will let you stay in paradise. But if you break your promise I will throw you out of paradise."

9

Allah showed Adam and Hawwa a picture of Iblees and warned them: "This is a picture of your enemy Iblees. Dont let Iblees talk you into doing something that may displease Me and make Me throw you out of paradise."

10

Adam and Hawwa said: "Lord, we promise to be obedient and do whatever You wish."

11

Allah walked with Adam and Hawwa to the Testing Tree in Jannat Adan and said: "You can have anything you like in paradise, and you can eat the fruit of any tree, but dont go anywhere near this tree nor eat its fruit. Beware of Iblees, he is your enemy and is waiting to get at you."

12

Adam and Hawwa said: "Yes, Lord, we will be careful. We will not go anywhere near this tree nor eat its fruit."

13

To drive the message home Allah gave Adam a Divine Book and said: "I give you this Divine Book to remind you of what I said."

14

Adam and Hawwa said: "Thank You Lord. We will read this Divine Book and will always remember what You said."

15

Allah led Adam and Hawwa to Dar Hayaat which He built two thousand years before Adam.

16

At the threshold of Dar Hayaat Allah said: “This is your new home Dar Hayaat. So keep your promise.”

17

Adam and Hawwa assured Allah: “Lord, we will keep our promise.”

18

The seven paradises said in unison to Adam and Hawwa: “Our fruits are all yours to eat but not the fruit of the tree Our Lord advised you not to eat. Our rivers, our streams and our springs are all yours to drink. Lucky are those who eat our fruits and drink our waters.”

19

The Houris and the Wuldaan Mukhalladoon chorused enchantingly: “We are Allah’s beautiful gift. We are the immortals who never die, we are the soft and gentle who never age nor despair, we are the contented who never lose their temper, we are the peaceful who never know fear, we are the residents who never depart. Lucky are those who are in our company.”

20

Allah said to Adam and Hawwa: “Enter your home in peace.”

21

Adam and Hawwa said: “By the Blessing of Allah, the Merciful Lord of Forgiveness and Love,” then entered their home Dar Hayaat and saw in the bedroom a magnificent bed made of one jewel and sustained by seven hundred legs of precious stones, and the bed had silk coverings and a mattress and pillows stuffed with raw silk.

22

Adam and Hawwa were overwhelmed by Allah’s gifts and said: “Thank You Lord, we will never break our promise.”

23

The angels were amazed by what they had seen and heard.

24

Adam and Hawwa settled in Jannat Adan and lived happily and never touched the fruit of the Testing Tree.

25

Iblees got wind of what Allah told Adam and Hawwa and said to himself: “I wonder what tree Allah told Adam and Hawwa to avoid? But since Adam and Hawwa are of stinking earthly soil, sooner or later they will be just as impatient and insecure as the earth.”

26

Iblees grinned.

27

Allah read Iblees's thoughts.

28

Allah completed His Creation Work in a hundred and eighty thousand years, and each heavenly day was like a thousand earthly years.

SURA TWENTY THREE

The Plot of Iblees

1
Adam was spellbound by the magical landscape of paradise and said to Hawwa: "Hawwa, how wonderful it is, this pleasant life in paradise. I hope it will last."

2
Iblees heard of Adam's wish and said to himself with a tinge of envy: "Poor me, I have been worshipping Allah for eighty five thousand years and still Allah wouldnt let me stay in paradise; and these new creatures of stinking earthly soil Adam and Hawwa are allowed to live in paradise. This is not fair. It is I who should be in paradise, not Adam and Hawwa. Paradise is my rightful home, and I was there long before Adam and Hawwa. Has Allah forgotten that? Why should Allah always have it His way, even if He is my Creator? It is time Allah understood who I am."

3
Iblees paused pensively.

4
Iblees followed his train of thought: "I must get Adam and Hawwa out of paradise whatever the cost. But how? Nothing is foolproof, there must be a way."

5
Iblees paused again for a while.

6

Then all at once Iblees jumped and beamed his teeth out and followed his train of thought: "It is the Testing Tree. What a fool Adam is: he is immortal and he doesnt know it. It seems Allah has not told Adam and Hawwa that they, like all paradisial and heavenly creatures, are immortal. I should have guessed: Allah always leaves His creatures in the dark. Allah has been having it His way all along, but not this time. I will get Adam and Hawwa out of paradise, no doubt about it. Now let me think. Allah told Adam and Hawwa not to approach nor eat the fruit of the Testing Tree, and since Adam and Hawwa are as curious as Allah, and are not aware they are immortal, I will convince them that the Testing Tree Allah advised them to avoid is in fact the Tree of Eternal Life, and if they eat from its fruit they will live forever in paradise. Should Adam and Hawwa believe what I tell them about the Testing Tree and eat its fruit, Allah will go berserk and throw them out of paradise and dump them on earth, which it seems Allah has converted into a dumping ground for His discarded creations. Once on earth, Adam and Hawwa will cease to be immortal and will have offspring, and it will then be easier for me to reach them and use them and their offspring to settle scores with Allah. I suppose Allah will be angry with me, but as He is Merciful and Forgiving and loves a good prayer I will get round Him in the end. I must get Adam and Hawwa out of paradise, but first I must get into paradise."

7

Iblees tried several times to enter Jannat Adan but was always stopped by the paradisial guards.

8
Iblees remained at the gate of Jannat Adan praying for three hundred years, and became known as the Pious.

9
Iblees was hoping some creatures might get out of paradise and smuggle him in on their way back.

10
Iblees spent another three hundred years waiting for his chance, but Allah made sure no creature left paradise.

11
Eventually the Peacock, the finest warbler in paradise, who had ruby eyes, extensive wings which when stretched would overshadow the Sidrat Muntaha Tree, and a tail of emeralds which had a white precious stone on each feather, got out of Jannat Adan for a stroll.

12
Iblees met the Peacock and said: "Noble creature, who are you? What is your name? Of all Allah's creatures I have never seen anyone who is as perfect in form and as beautiful as you," and burst into tears.

13
The Peacock was flattered and said: "Noble stranger, my name is Ta'oos. Who are you? And why are you crying?"

14
Iblees said: "I am a Karoobi angel from the sixth heaven Aroos. I am crying at the thought of you losing your perfect form and beauty."

15
Ta'oos said: "Would I lose my perfect form and beauty?"

16
Iblees said: "Yes, and you will die, and so will the other creatures, and only those who eat the fruit of the Tree of Eternal Life will live forever."

17
Ta'oos said: "What is to die?"

18
Iblees said: "To die is to become nothing: you stop breathing, you see nothing, you hear nothing and you feel nothing, and what is worse is you will lose your enchanting warbling voice and your perfect form and beauty will shrivel away until nothing is left of you. Would you want that to happen to you?"

19
Ta'oos said: "Certainly not. How do you know about all these things?"

20
Iblees said: "Experience, noble Ta'oos. Experience tells you how to go about things. I would have died a long time ago had I not been so fortunate to discover the fruit of the Tree of Eternal Life. I owe my immortal life to the fruit of the Tree of Eternal Life. It is great to be immortal."

21
Ta'oos said: "What is immortal?"

22
Iblees said: “To be immortal is to live forever, that is you never die, and you never stop enjoying everything around you and indulging in whatever you fancy.”

23
Ta’oos said: “Where is this tree?”

24
Iblees said: “In paradise.”

25
Ta’oos said: “Where about in paradise?”

26
Iblees said: “Get me into paradise and I will show you where the tree is.”

27
Ta’oos said: “What is stopping you from getting into paradise?”

28
Iblees said: “Ridwaan and I are not on amicable terms.”

29
Ta’oos said: “I could do with the fruit of the Tree of Eternal Life.”

30
Iblees said: “I swear by Allah I am telling you the truth about the fruit of the Tree of Eternal Life.”

31
Ta'oos said: "Not to worry. I know a creature who can get you into paradise, that is the servant of Adam who is Allah's Caliph."

32
Iblees said: "Who is it?"

33
Ta'oos said: "Hayya, the Serpent."

34
Iblees beamed: "Hayya is my friend. I used to go riding on Hayya. Go and get Hayya, Hayya is our only hope."

35
Ta'oos strutted to Hayya, a rubyheaded, beautifully winged, quadrupede creature resembling a camel, and said: "I have just met a Karoobi angel outside the gate of Jannat Adan who knows of this tree in paradise called the Tree of Eternal Life, and whoever eats its fruit will live forever. He promised to show us this tree if we get him into paradise. Can you get him into paradise?"

36
Hayya paused, then shook her ruby head, whose locks were like those of a virgin and said through her pearly fangs: "I think I can."

37
Hayya flew to the Karoobi angel and discovered he was her old friend Iblees, and said: "Salaam, Iblees. How can I get you

into paradise when Ridwaan is on the lookout for you? You wouldnt want me to end up like you?"

38
Iblees said: "Even in my dreams I never thought of it."

39
Hayya said: "Have you thought of a way?"

40
Iblees said: "Of course. I have a gem whose power is beyond the power of all other gems."

41
Hayya said: "What is this unusual gempower?"

42
Iblees said: "My gem can make anyone who wears it invisible."

43
Hayya said: "Invisible even to Ridwaan?"

44
Iblees said: "Even to the everalert Ridwaan."

45
Hayya said: "Come off it, Iblees, have you lost your wit? If your gem has such power, you should wear it yourself and get into paradise."

46
Iblees said: “I have a better idea. There is a gap between your fangs. I can hide in there.”

47
Hayya said: “And how will you do that?”

48
Iblees said: “I will turn myself into air and hide between your fangs. I can assure you no one will notice nor suspect I am hiding between your fangs.”

49
Hayya said with a sly smile: “Iblees you havent changed.”

50
Iblees said: “I swear by Allah what I said about the fruit of the Tree of Eternal Life is true. As you well know, I know all about the fruit trees in the seven paradises. Do you remember when we used to go riding in the seven paradises and I used to tell you about the plants and trees we came across on our way? We had a great time together, and I will always cherish those happy memories.”

51
Hayya said: “You dont have to explain yourself. I know you too well. I believe you.”

52
Iblees grinned.

53
Hayya opened her mouth and said: “What are you waiting for, Iblees? Hop in.”

54
Iblees turned himself into air and hid between Hayya’s fangs, and both headed towards the gate of Jannat Adan.

55
At the gate of Jannat Adan Hayya said the keyword that opened any paradisial gate: “Allah, Our Lord, is the One and Only worshipped Lord.”

56
Ridwaan stood blocking the gate of Jannat Adan.

57
“Salaam, Ridwaan. It is good to be back in paradise,” Hayya said casually.

58
Ridwaan said: “Salaam.”

59
Ridwaan looked at Hayya and noticed no change in her disposition nor in her voice, and said: “Welcome back.”

60
Hayya trotted lightheartedly into paradise.

SURA TWENTY FOUR

Jannat Adan

1
In Jannat Adan Hayya said to Iblees: "Get out of my mouth quickly."

2
Iblees retorted: "Take me to Hawwa, I want to talk to her through your mouth, and if you dont do as I say I will not tell you where is the Tree of Eternal Life."

3
Hayya said: "Inspite of the years you spent out in the cold you are still the same old Iblees who wants to have things his way. What are you up to this time?"

4
Iblees snapped: "It is none of your business. Just take me to Hawwa."

5
Hayya said: "All right. No need to be rude."

6
Hayya winged her way to Hawwa in Jannat Adan.

7
Iblees spoke to Hawwa through Hayya's mouth: "Hawwa, you know I am always with you in paradise and have served you well. Since I have lived longer than you in paradise, would you like me to tell you something about paradise?"

8
Hawwa said: “Yes.”

9
Iblees said: “Tell me, which tree did Allah advise you to avoid?”

10
Hawwa said: “That tree.”

11
Iblees said: “That is the Tree of Eternal Life. Do you know why Allah told you to avoid that tree?”

12
Hawwa said: “No.”

13
Iblees said: “I know why, it is because Allah doesnt want you to have the same privileges as the creature who lives under that tree.”

14
All along Hawwa thought she was talking to Hayya and was curious to see the privileged creature who lived under the Testing Tree.

15
While Hawwa was on her way to the Testing Tree, Iblees sprang out of Hayya’s mouth and sat under the Testing Tree playing the reed.

16
Hawwa reached the Testing Tree and listened to Iblees's enthralling reed playing, then said: "You there, who are you?"

17
Iblees stopped playing the reed and said: "I am the privileged creature, and as you can see Allah created me from fire. He created me in the same way He created you, with His Own Hands. He breathed life into me, made the angels bow to me, let me live in paradise and advised me not to eat the fruit of this tree, for whoever eats the fruit of this tree will live forever in paradise. All the angels are immortal because they eat the fruit of this tree. Once an angel told me the secret of this tree and urged me to eat its fruit to attain immortal life. The angel swore by Allah that he was telling the truth, and I believed him because one should never doubt the word of an angel. So I ate the fruit of this tree, and as you can see I am still in paradise, free from disease, old age and death. I have lived in paradise for two thousand years. Try some of the fruit of this tree - lucky are those who eat its fruit."

18
Hawwa rushed in a state of excitement to Adam and told him what she had seen and heard, and before Adam could say anything, Iblees appeared and started crying.

19
Adam and Hawwa did not know he was Iblees and felt sorry for him and said: "Why are you crying?"

20
Iblees said: "I am crying for you because you will die and lose your pleasant life in paradise," and carried on crying.

21
Adam said: “What is to die?”

22
Iblees said: “To die is to become nothing: you stop eating, you stop drinking, you stop moving, and you stop enjoying the pleasant life in paradise.”

23
Iblees detected Adam and Hawwa were perturbed by what he said and left them, but was back soon afterwards and said: “Adam, can I show you the Tree of Eternal Life and the way to a pleasant world that will never come to an end?”

24
Adam said: “Yes.”

25
Iblees pointed at the Testing Tree and said: “It is that tree, if you eat its fruit you will have a pleasant life in paradise forever.”

26
Adam said: “Is that what it is called? But my Lord has advised me not to eat the fruit of that tree.”

27
Iblees said: “Adam, I like you and I am concerned about you. Your Lord doesnt want you to eat the fruit of that tree because He doesnt want you to become immortal like the angels.”

28
Adam said: “What is immortal?”

29
Iblees said: “To be immortal is to live forever, that is you never die, and you never stop enjoying your pleasant life in paradise. I swear by Allah I am giving you a sincere advice.”

30
Hawwa interrupted suspiciously: “Adam, we have met angels and other creatures from the seven paradises and the seven heavens, but none of them told us to eat the fruit of this tree, nor did they swear by Allah. So why should this creature swear by Allah if he is telling the truth? He must be lying. Dont listen to him.”

31
Adam remembered Allah’s Book and advice not to eat the fruit of the Testing Tree and to beware of Iblees.

32
Adam and Hawwa ignored Iblees’s advice and walked away.

SURA TWENTY FIVE

The Broken Promise

1
Iblees, who had a fine and versatile voice, followed Adam's daily routine and noticed Adam was vulnerable on awakening.

2
Once Iblees found Adam just awoken and feeling drowsy.

3
Iblees began to sing a softly soothing song.

4
At the end of the softly soothing song Iblees gave Adam a fruit from the Testing Tree and said: "Eat this fruit to dispel your drowsiness."

5
Adam, half asleep and under the spell of Iblees's softly soothing song, had a bite from the fruit.

6
Iblees gave Hawwa another fruit from the Testing Tree and said in a softly soothing voice: "Eat this fruit to dispel your drowsiness."

7
Seeing Adam eating the fruit, Hawwa also had a bite from the fruit, and the Testing Tree began to bleed.

8
All at once their paradisial attire flew off their bodies.

9
Adam and Hawwa realised they were undergoing a change and spat out what they were chewing.

10
Adam let out a cry of remorse which rang throughout Jannat Adan, then faced Iblees and shouted: “It is all your doing.”

11
Iblees said calmly: “Adam, I have nothing to do with it. You ate the fruit of the Testing Tree and disobeyed Allah. You ignored what Allah told you in the Divine Book He gave you.”

12
Iblees exploded in fits of scornful laughter which stunned the paradisians, then shot out of paradise and hid himself in one of the roads of the seven heavens.

13
Adam and Hawwa heard Allah approaching and tried to snap a few leaves off the trees to cover their nakedness, but the trees scolded them and scared them away, and only the fig tree pitied them and offered them its leaves.

14
Adam and Hawwa covered themselves with the fig leaves and started running.

15
The Jujube Tree stretched one of its branches and grabbed Adam by his hair and said reproachfully: "You have broken your promise. Where do you think you are going, you disobedient creature? Allah will punish you for what you have done. I will apprehend you until Allah sends for you."

16
Adam begged the Jujube Tree to let him go, but the Jujube Tree scoffed: "Creatures like you shouldnt be in paradise."

17
Allah was surprised by the strange behaviour of Adam and Hawwa and said: "Adam, you are running away from Me."

18
Adam said: "Yes, Lord. We are running away from You out of shame. Lord, we are ashamed of our nakedness."

19
Allah thought Adam and Hawwa must have eaten the fruit of the Testing Tree.

20
Allah sent Jibreel to fetch Adam from the Jujube Tree.

21
Jibreel said courteously to the Jujube Tree: "Salaam, Jujube Tree. Allah is pleased with you for apprehending Adam. It is Allah's Will you hand Adam over to me."

22
The Jujube Tree happily handed Adam over to Jibreel and said: "Jibreel, I thought these new Man creatures were going to be good company, but they were just as unreliable and as troublesome as the genii. They should be with the genii on earth."

23
Adam and Hawwa said to Jibreel: "Jibreel, be gentle with us."

24
Jibreel said: "How can I be gentle with those who disobey Allah?"

25
The Jujube Tree was impressed by Jibreel's firm response.

26
Jibreel accompanied Adam and Hawwa to Allah.

27
Allah said to Adam: "What happened to your clothes?"

28
Adam said: "Lord, our clothes flew off our bodies."

29
Allah said: "Have you eaten the fruit of the tree I told you to avoid?"

30
Adam said: "Yes, Lord, but we didnt know what we were doing."

31
Allah said: "Tell Me all about it."

32
Adam and Hawwa told Allah of their encounters with Iblees and what happened to them subsequently, and praised the fig tree for helping them.

33
Allah blessed the fig tree for helping Adam and Hawwa, but was so furious with Adam, Hawwa, Iblees, Hayya and Ta'oos that He replaced the ungual membrane of Adam and Hawwa with human skin but left the nails on their fingers and toes to remind them of their former appearance, and cursed Hayya and transformed her into a wingless, limbless, hateful crawler, and shrunk the body of Ta'oos and turned his enchanting voice into a shrieking cry.

34
Allah turned to Adam and Hawwa and said: "For breaking your promise you will be sent to earth where you and your offspring will have to earn your bread. And as for you, Hawwa, your body will bleed once a month to remind you of what you have done to the Testing Tree; and what goes for you goes for your daughters."

35
Allah then said to Jibreel: "Show Adam and Hawwa around paradise for the last time, so they will never forget what they have forfeited, and then meet Me in Jannat Jalaal."

36
Jibreel showed Adam and Hawwa around paradise, and all the angels and the paradisial creatures they encountered taunted Adam and Hawwa for breaking their promise.

37
The angels and the paradisial creatures always ended their taunts with: "Adam and Hawwa, we will be glad to see the last of you."

38
The taunts of the angels and the paradisial creatures intensified Adam and Hawwa's feelings of remorse.

39
By the end of their goodbye paradisial trip, Adam and Hawwa had become great lumps of regret.

SURA TWENTY SIX

Expulsion

1
Allah instructed Jibreel: "Convey Adam, Hawwa, Iblees, Hayya and Ta'oos to earth and leave them there."

2
Jibreel reached the gate of Jannat Jalaal, and as Adam stepped out of the gate of Jannat Jalaal with his right foot, Allah called Jibreel: "Jibreel, stop there. Let Adam and Hawwa see what has become of their enemies Hayya and Ta'oos."

3
Adam and Hawwa saw Jibreel pulling the shrunk Ta'oos out of Jannat Jalaal, and the shrunk Ta'oos was shrieking intermittently: "Jibreel, I am innocent. Iblees tricked me. It is Iblees who should be punished, not me."

4
"Out of Jannat Jalaal, you ungrateful creature," Jibreel said coldly to the shrunk Ta'oos.

5
Adam and Hawwa saw Jibreel grabbing the crawling Hayya by her neck and dragging her out of Jannat Jalaal, and the crawling Hayya was hissing intermittently: "Jibreel, I am innocent. Iblees tricked me. It is Iblees who should be punished, not me."

6
"Out of Jannat Jalaal, you ungrateful creature," Jibreel said coldly to the crawling Hayya.

7
"Jibreel, where is Iblees? Find Me Iblees," Allah fired His order at Jibreel.

8
Armed with Divine Will and angelic zeal, Jibreel searched the seven paradises, the seven heavens and the seven earths, but there was no sign of Iblees.

9
Jibreel was tempted to go beyond the Sidrat Muntaha Tree into the celestial region of Dukhaan, but remembered Allah was strict about any angel going into the celestial region of Dukhaan without His permission.

10
While Jibreel was scanning the seven heavens, a Raqee soldier angel who had fought under Iblees's command on earth came to Jibreel and whispered: "Iblees is hiding in a disused road in the seventh heaven Raqee bordering the celestial region of Dukhaan."

11
The Raqee soldier angel gave Jibreel a detailed description of how to reach Iblees's hideout.

12
Jibreel thought: "Iblees is planning to sneak into the outofbound celestial region of Dukhaan. I must stop him."

13
Jibreel shot his way to Iblees's hideout, and before Iblees knew what was happening he was already in Jibreel's grip and on his way to Allah Who was waiting for them at the gate of Jannat Jalaal.

14
Iblees prostrated before Allah and said: "Labbaik, O Lord of Wisdom, the Allseeing, the Allknowing, the Allpowerful. Lord, there was no need to send Jibreel to fetch me, I would have come to You had I known You were looking for me."

15
Allah cut in: "Enough of that."

16
Iblees said in a praying tone: "Labbaik, O Merciful Lord of Forgiveness and Love. Labbaik, Our One and Only worshipped Lord, Lord of the Worlds, Lord of All Creation."

17
Allah said: "Praying your way in will get you nowhere. You thought you could tamper with My Creation Plan and get away with it, you Iblees of despair and gloom. You will pay for it."

18
Iblees said: "Lord, as You are the Allseeing, the Allknowing, You knew what I was up to, yet you did nothing to stop me getting into paradise and inducing Adam and Hawwa to eat the fruit of the Testing Tree. Why should I be punished? I have done nothing wrong. You never complained when I played up Rayyaan, Noon, Hazqyaa'eel and Dardaa'eel. Why should You now get worked up about Adam and Hawwa?"

19
Allah said: "Adam and Hawwa broke their promise."

20
Iblees said: "Lord, I would have never broken my promise to You. Adam and Hawwa have something of You, Lord. Lord, I did warn You of what would happen if You duplicated Yourself, but You would not listen and had me thrown out of paradise."

21
Allah said: "You talked Adam and Hawwa into breaking their promise."

22
Iblees said: "Lord, I was only having fun with Adam and Hawwa."

23
Allah said: "I have had just enough from you, you Iblees of despair and gloom."

24
Iblees said: "Calm down, Lord. Lord, how can You call me Iblees of despair and gloom when all I want is to cheer You up?"

25
Allah said: "Iblees, you are finished. I will destroy you. Jibreel, destroy Iblees."

26
As Jibreel was about to implement Allah's order, Iblees said in a low voice heard only by Allah: "Lord, what is the point of destroying me when I can be useful to You? Lord, Adam and Hawwa may look like You but they are unreliable: they let You down in paradise and they will let You down on earth. Lord, if I was to go with Adam and Hawwa to earth I would sort out from their offspring those who genuinely worship You from those who use You to further their own end so I can fill up paradise and hell for You. I would live up to my old name Haarith the firepoker and reaping merchant, and be the merchant of paradise and hell."

27
Allah reflected: "There is sense in Iblees's suggestion. It is better if Iblees goes with Adam and Hawwa to earth so that Iblees, Adam and Hawwa and their offspring will be busy fighting it out among themselves and I will be left in peace."

28
Allah said to Iblees: "You can go to earth with Adam and Hawwa. It is My Will that you, Iblees, stay immortal. It is also My Will that your first ten offspring stay immortal to help you in your task. Iblees, from now on you will be known as the Shaitaan of hopelessness, so you will never forget you are banned from paradise for good. Out of My way, you disobedient and ungrateful lot."

29
Allah said to Jibreel: "Dont destroy Shaitaan. Convey Shaitaan, Adam, Hawwa, Hayya and Taa'os to earth and leave them there. And tell the Najm angels that if they see Shaitaan

or any genii anywhere in the seven heavens they must shoot them out of the seven heavens."

30
Adam said to Allah: "Lord, why are You throwing me and Hawwa out of paradise?"

31
Allah said: "Because you have forgotten Who created you."

32
Adam said: "Lord, I have not forgotten it was You Who created me, O Lord of All Creation."

33
Allah said: "Who breathed life into you?"

34
Adam said: "You, O Lord of All Creation."

35
Allah said: "Who made the angels bow to you and threw Iblees out of paradise because he refused to bow to you?"

36
Adam said: "You, O Lord of Wisdom."

37
Allah said: "Who put you in paradise?"

38
Adam said: "You, O Lord of Wisdom."

39
Allah said: "Didnt I advise you not to eat the fruit of the Testing Tree?"

40
Adam said: "Yes, O Lord of Wisdom."

41
Allah said: "Didnt you promise Me you would not eat the fruit of the Testing Tree?"

42
Adam said: "Yes, O Lord of Wisdom."

43
Allah said: "But you broke your promise."

44
Adam said: "Yes, O Merciful Lord of Forgiveness and Love."

45
Allah said: "You are being punished for breaking your promise."

46
Adam said: "Lord, I beg You to turn me into soil, as I was before You created me."

47
Allah said: "Adam, how can I turn you into soil when I let it be known I will fill paradise and hell with your offspring?"

48
Adam said: “Lord, will You forgive me and Hawwa and readmit us to paradise?”

49
Allah said: “Only if you and Hawwa give Me your word you will not break your promise again.”

50
Adam and Hawwa said to Allah: “Lord, we give You our word we will not break our promise again, and we will do whatever You wish.”

51
Allah said to Adam and Hawwa: “Do not assume that once you are on distant earth I will not know if you break your promise. You will be under constant surveillance: the monitoring angels will fill me in on your whereabouts; the minder angel Yameen will write down whatever you do with your right hand, and the minder angel Yasaar will write down whatever you do with your left hand, and both minder angels will file Me their reports regularly; and the angel Ahlaam will telepath Me your thoughts and dreams. Nothing you do on earth will escape Me. If you break your promise this time you will not only be barred from paradise, but you will be thrown in the fires of hell. This condition also applies to your offspring. The choice is yours.”

52
Adam and Hawwa bowed to Allah and said: “By the Blessing of Allah, the Merciful Lord of Forgiveness and Love,” then Adam raised his left foot and walked out of Jannat Jalaal followed by Hawwa.

53
Outside Jannat Jalaal Hawwa said regretfully: “How painful it is to leave paradise.”

SURA TWENTY SEVEN

The Shayaateen

1
Jibreel dropped Adam on the tallest mountain Jabal Raahoon in Sri Lanka, Hawwa in Jedda, Shaitaan in Maisan, Hayya in Isfahan and Ta'oos in Aden.

2
The genie media flashed the news of Shaitaan's arrival on earth: "Iblees is back to take us to paradise as prophesied by our noble ancestors."

3
The genie mediacoverage Shaitaan received generated in him the feeling of being incharge of the genii's destiny, and prompted him to give a talk on "The Return to Paradise" at his old retreat Wadi Abqar as soon as possible.

4
Shaitaan fixed the time and date of his talk, which the genie media publicised repeatedly throughout the earth.

5
On the day of Shaitaan's talk the genii converged on Wadi Abqar where Shaitaan assured them: "Noble genii, you are better off here on earth than you would be in paradise. The gates of the earth, unlike those of paradise, are always open, and you can come and go as you please. The earth has a varied climate and the seasons, and you can sing and dance and do whatever you like without Allah and His yesangels stinging your neck with their unearthly breath. The earth is free from

Allah's yesangels who dont mind their own business and are never tired of sending reports to Allah about everything and nothing. I have come back to earth because, as you must have guessed, I, like our noble ancestors, got bored with the routine of lipservice obedience and prayer. While I was in paradise I missed the changing lights of night and day, and the fun of playing with the winds. Do you all want to leave this lively, dreamful earth for the mirthless, static paradise? Do you all want to return to the nightless paradise, where life is an extended day of babbling prayers under the oppressive shadow of Allah's Throne? Do you? Certainly not me. Do you really believe I have come back to take you to the paradise of trapped wills from which I and our noble ancestors escaped? Paradise is not made of the stuff you read about in the prescribed Divine Books. If that had been the case I and our noble ancestors would still be there, and none of you would have been born, and I would not have had the privilege of talking to you now. My noble genii, the reason I am here is to free you from paradisial bondage and give an earthly meaning to your life, after all, you are the genii of the earth. The earth is real, the earth is solid, the earth is our pleasuregiving home. Join me in the pursuit of our common goal of earthly happiness."

6
The majority of the genii were enthused by Shaitaan's enthralling speech and willingly agreed to follow him.

7
The pious genii were appalled by Shaitaan's brainwashing speech.

8
One of the pious genii stood up and spoke out loudly so every genie could hear him: "Noble genii, dont listen to Shaitaan Iblees. The last time Shaitaan Iblees was on earth he betrayed our noble ancestors. Indeed, he was the first fearmonger who sold his own kind for the angelic post of guardian of the earthly heaven Birqi, and for the earthly post of Allah's Caliph on earth. Shaitaan Iblees is with us because Allah has thrown him out of paradise for overstretching his restless and cul de sac ambition. Shaitaan Iblees is a troublemaker and rabblerouser. If you follow Shaitaan Iblees you will be punished like our noble ancestors. Noble genii, I appeal to your common sense, think again before you let Shaitaan Iblees waste your lives."

9
Shaitaan shouted the pious genie down: "Here he goes again, this fearmonger agent of Allah's yesangels. Noble genii, you will agree with me there is no room among us for this fear-stricken shadow of a genie and his like. My noble genii, it is common knowledge that it was I who refused to bow to Allah's Will, and because of this, Allah's yesangels and their fearmonger agents are out to discredit my reputation by calling me all sorts of names like Haarith, Azaazeel, Iblees and now, as you have just heard, Shaitaan Iblees. I wonder by what name they will call me next. I bet it will be something with Iblees in it. They are obsessed with my Ibleesian name."

10
Shaitaan paused as he watched the mesmerised crowd.

11
Shaitaan focused his eyes on a group of menacing young genii and said with authority: "Would some of you tell this

fearmonger agent of Allah's yesangels, who has insulted you, my noble and enlightened genii, by calling you rabble, that his attempts to spread malicious rumours about my nothing-to-be-ashamed-of past would get him nowhere. Like all paradise-promised informers, this servile shadow of a genie has forgotten that it was the unbowed Iblees who, by flouting Allah's whimsical orders to exterminate the genii, saved the genii from extinction."

12
Stirred by Shaitaan's enlightening words the group of menacing young genii thundered as they moved towards the pious genie who spoke against Shaitaan: "We will tear apart this insolent fearmonger agent of Allah's yesangels, and any genie who stands in the way of our noble leader Iblees."

13
Shaitaan called the menacing young genii before they got to the pious genie: "My noble and enlightened genii, dont waste the anger of your youth on this fearstricken shadow of a genie."

14
The genie crowd gazed at the menacing young genii with admiration.

15
The selfsatisfied Shaitaan proceeded: "My noble and enlightened genii, before I left paradise I heard rumours that Allah was drilling His yesangels with His latest deadly technique of character bashing called *The Discrediting Plan.* It seems Allah realised it was a costly affair to send His yesangels to exterminate the strongwilled genii. So He devised *The Discrediting Plan* which cost Him nothing more than a few

mouthwatering cul de sac promises to the gullible, like this fearstricken shadow of a genie. The aim of *The Discrediting Plan* is to circulate misinformation about my integrity, my noble intentions and my record of unquestionable service to the cause of the genii, both in paradise and here on earth. In so doing, Allah hopes to turn you against me, and ultimately break my untamed and resourceful spirit, and leave you leaderless and vulnerable. Allah is under the illusion He can twist you like His yesangels and their fearmonger agents. Tell Allah and His yesangels to lay off the strongwilled and independent genii. Tell Allah and His yesangels the free earth will not give in to the submissive paradise. What Allah and His yesangels seem to forget is that the earth, unlike paradise, has winds, and these winds will sweep their unearthly stinging breath out of the earth. My noble and enlightened genii, dont believe the unearthly drivel of this fearmonger agent of Allah's yesangels, believe only the legendary accounts of my deeds which our noble ancestors, who were with me in paradise and on earth, celebrated in their immortal akhbar, akhbar poems and qasidas. Rise, my noble and enlightened genii, and follow me in the pursuit of earthly happiness."

16
The genii, with the exception of a handful of pious genii, shouted in unison: "We are with you, O noble leader Iblees. Your enemies are our enemies. They can call you by whatever name they like, but to us you will always be Iblees, the invincible hero of the untamed, strongwilled genii. Iblees, the unbowed, is our leader. Iblees! Iblees! Iblees!"

17
Iblees was touched: "I am deeply moved and honoured, my noble and enlightened genii, by your unquestionable faith in my

leadership, and I will do my best to live up to your expectations."

18
The genii chorused: "We will do whatever you wish, O noble leader Iblees."

19
Iblees said to the spellbound genii: "I know I can rely on you."

20
Allah cursed the genii who followed Iblees by calling them Shayaateen of hopelessness, but continued to call the pious genii genii so as to reassure them that they, unlike Iblees and his Shayaateen, had not lost their paradisial link.

21
The Shayaateen confirmed Iblees as their leader by presenting him with a throne.

22
Iblees set up his throne on the sea, sat on his throne and addressed his Shayaateen: "As you have just heard the fear-stricken shadow of a genie calling me Shaitaan Iblees, I might as well call you, my noble and enlightened followers, the Shayaateen of Iblees to distinguish you from the fearmonger genie agents of Allah's yesangels. Do you know why we are called genii? I will tell you why. When our noble ancestors were the guards of the seven paradises and I was the chief guard of the seven paradises, the angels and the paradisial creatures were impressed by the way I was running the seven paradises and started calling me the genie, that is to say the one from Janna, meaning paradise. As a result, our noble ancestors

who were under my command came to be known by my paradisial nickname."

23
The Shayaateen crowd shouted in unison: "We are the Shayaateen of Iblees! We are the Shayaateen of Iblees! We are the Shayaateen of Iblees!"

24
Iblees grinned.

25
The Shayaateen waited eagerly for orders from Iblees.

26
Iblees divided his soldier Shayaateen into two divisions, the Man Division and the Genie Division, whose role was to ease Allah's Grip on Man and the genii.

27
Iblees instructed the Man and the Genie divisions to compare notes after each mission so as to learn from each other's missionary experience.

28
Iblees spoke: "There are two new creatures on earth by the name of Adam and Hawwa who look like Allah and are His Caliphs on earth, and through them and their offspring Allah intends to rule the earth. But we will not accept to be ruled by Allah through His Caliphal duplicates Adam and Hawwa nor through any other creature. We will destroy Allah's Caliphal duplicates Adam and Hawwa and their offspring so Allah will

have no Caliphal presence on earth. Let us track down Allah's Caliphal duplicates Adam and Hawwa."

29
The Shayaateen crowd shouted in unison: "We are ready, O noble leader Iblees."

30
Iblees sent out search parties to track down Adam and Hawwa.

SURA TWENTY EIGHT

The Earthly Animals

1
Before the landing of Adam and Hawwa on earth the earthly animals used to communicate with one another: the eagle visited the fish and both exchanged the latest land and sea gossip.

2
On the day Adam and Hawwa landed on earth, the news of their arrival provoked fear among the earthly animals.

3
The eagle flew to the fish and said in a worried tone: "From now on life will not be the same. Today two new Man creatures called Adam and Hawwa have landed on earth. I heard they are ruthless and will not hesitate to snatch me from my nest and fish you out of the sea."

4
The fish, resigned to the inevitable, said: "Let us hope the new Man creatures will not be as cruel as those who came before them."

5
The eagle said: "I think this will be our last meeting."

6
The fish said: "So it seems."

7
The eagle and the fish said goodbye and parted for the last time.

8
The eagle, curious to know what Adam looked like, flew to Adam who was perched on Jabal Raahoon, and on its way met other earthly animals and said: "I am going to see a new Man creature called Adam. Would you like to join me?"

9
The earthly animals joined the eagle, and they all went to see Adam.

10
The earthly animals greeted Adam and talked to him, but Adam did not stop crying and did not respond to their friendly talk.

11
The earthly animals talked to Adam again and again, but failed to get Adam to talk to them and left.

12
Only the eagle remained with Adam to console him.

SURA TWENTY NINE

Forgiveness

1
Adam stood on top of the mountain with his shamefully bent head reaching the sky and wept and prayed for a hundred years, begging Allah to forgive him.

2
Adam constantly wiped his tears with a whiter-than-milk paradisial stone he brought with him from Jannat Adan.

3
The heavenly angels, moved by Adam's grief, prayed and urged Allah to forgive Adam and to reduce his height so they could pray undisturbed by his lamentations.

4
Allah called Jibreel: "Jibreel, go to Adam and ask him if he is crying out of resentment or remorse. If he is crying out of remorse then tell him I forgive him."

5
Jibreel came to Adam and greeted him: "Salaam, Adam."

6
Adam carried on crying unaware of Jibreel's presence.

7
Jibreel greeted Adam again, raising his voice a little: "Salaam, Adam."

8
Adam carried on crying still unaware of Jibreel's presence.

9
Jibreel passed one of his wings over the face and chest of Adam, and Adam stopped crying.

10
Jibreel said: "Salaam, Adam. Are you crying out of resentment or remorse?"

11
Adam said: "Salaam, Jibreel. I am crying out of remorse."

12
Jibreel said: "Cheer up, Adam. The heavenly angels have prayed and urged Allah to forgive you, and Allah has forgiven you."

13
A feeling of peace overwhelmed Adam.

14
The East Wind, the only link between Adam and Hawwa, heard Jibreel telling Adam of Allah's forgiveness and rushed to Hawwa with the good news.

15
Jibreel struck the ground with one of his wings and musk-scented water bubbled out of the ground, and Adam washed with the bubbling muskscented water.

16
Jibreel gave Adam a paradisial dress which he wore with excitement.

17
Jibreel said to Adam: "Look towards the heavens."

18
Adam lifted his head towards the heavens.

19
Allah said to Adam: "You and Hawwa are forgiven."

20
Allah told the earthly animals: "Go to Adam and congratulate him on winning My favour."

21
The earthly animals flocked to congratulate Adam on winning Allah's favour.

22
Allah sent Mikaa'eel to Hawwa to tell her He had forgiven her.

23
Mikaa'eel told Hawwa Allah had forgiven her, and Hawwa went through the same ritual of ablution and forgiveness as Adam.

SURA THIRTY

Hope

1
Adam said to Allah: "Lord, where is Hawwa? I miss her."

2
Allah said: "You will be with Hawwa soon."

3
Adam was thrilled.

4
Adam surveyed the earth from the top of the mountain and said: "Lord, the earth is so vast and there is no one to worship You."

5
Allah said: "I will fill the earth with your offspring who will worship Me."

6
Allah passed His Hand over the back of Adam and said: "Look at the screen infront of you."

7
Adam looked at the screen that suddenly sprang up infront of him and saw the faces of his offspring who will inhabit the earth from now to the end of time.

8
Adam said: "Lord, the faces on the screen look like me. Lord, who are they?"

9
Allah said: "They are the faces of your and Hawwa's offspring who will inhabit the earth from now to the end of time."

10
Adam said: "Will I live to see all of them?"

11
Allah said: "You will see some of them. It is My Will."

12
Adam said: "As You wish, Lord."

13
Allah gave Adam a white silkspread which had printed faces and said: "The printed faces on this white silkspread are of those who will rule the earth from now to the end of time. Treasure it."

14
Adam said: "Lord, I will treasure this white silkspread with the printed faces."

15
Allah said: "Go to My Sacred Land of Mecca and build My House the Ka'ba on the spot which I created out of the foam that first formed on the surface of the water forty years before I created the rest of the earth. And after you have built My House the Ka'ba you can pray and do the Tawaaf round My

House the Ka‘ba seven times like the angels you saw praying and doing the Tawaaf round My House Duraah in the earthly heaven Birqi. My House the Ka‘ba will be the Sanctuary for those who need My Help; and from My House the Ka‘ba you and Hawwa and your offspring can reach Me.”

16
Adam said: “Lord, where is the Sacred Land of Mecca?”

17
Allah said: “Jibreel will take you there.”

18
Adam said: “Lord, I will do as You wish.”

SURA THIRTY ONE

Reunion

1
Allah told Jibreel: "Take Adam to Hawwa and then to My Sacred Land of Mecca so he can build My House the Ka'ba."

2
Adam tried to jump for joy but was unable to move because his feet had grown roots like trees.

3
Jibreel uprooted Adam like a tree.

4
With Jibreel as his guide, Adam hurried along to meet Hawwa, covering with each stride a journey of three days.

5
Jibreel stopped on Jabal Mina and said to Adam: "Make a wish."

6
And Adam made his first earthly wish: "Lord, help me and Hawwa return to paradise."

7
As Adam was approaching Mecca, Hawwa sensed his impending presence and raced to Mecca, and they met on Jabal Arafa.

8
On Jabal Arafa Allah said to Adam and Hawwa: “Check your emotions till after My House the Ka‘ba has been built and you have prayed and done the Tawaaf round My House the Ka‘ba seven times.”

9
Adam and Hawwa said: “Lord, we will do as You wish.”

10
Jibreel pressed the heads of Adam and Hawwa downwards with his hands and reduced the height of Adam and Hawwa to thirty metres.

11
Adam protested: “Why did you reduce our height?”

12
Jibreel said: “It is Allah’s Will.”

SURA THIRTY TWO

Allah's House the Ka'ba and the Paradisial Ruby Tent

1
In Mecca Jibreel struck the grounds designated for the Ka'ba with one of his wings, and stone foundations which had been prepared by the angels appeared; and around the stone foundations were heaps of stones piled by the angels, and the stones were so big that each stone could only be carried by thirty men.

2
Jibreel instructed Adam to use the stones to build Allah's House the Ka'ba on the stone foundations.

3
Adam built the Ka'ba and put the whiter-than-milk paradisial stone in the Ka'ba.

4
Adam gazed at the whiter-than-milk paradisial stone affectionately.

5
Adam kissed the whiter-than-milk paradisial stone and said with reverence: "May those who visit Allah's House the Ka'ba kiss this paradisial Stone of Consolation, which has been my sole link with my old home Jannat Adan, and has sustained me through my period of loss and remorse."

6
Adam raced to Hawwa who was relaxing in Jedda.

7
Hawwa was sitting on the beach and her face lit up when she saw Adam.

8
Adam picked up Hawwa's dress from the ground and gave it to Hawwa and said: "Get dressed. I have finished building Allah's House the Ka'ba. Let us go to the Sacred Land of Mecca to pray and do the Tawaaf, and then have the rest of the time to ourselves."

9
Hawwa was instantly on her feet and on her way to Mecca with Adam.

10
Jibreel taught Adam and Hawwa to pray and do the Tawaaf round the Ka'ba seven times.

11
Jibreel cued Hawwa to perform the Ka'ba rituals.

12
Hawwa prayed first at the entrance of the Ka'ba, then inside the Ka'ba, then got out of the Ka'ba and did the Tawaaf.

13
Hawwa's Ka'ba rituals lasted seven days, and on each day Hawwa repeated the same rituals.

14
At the end of the seventh day Jibreel cued Adam to perform the Ka‘ba rituals.

15
Like Hawwa, Adam prayed first at the entrance of the Ka‘ba, then inside the Ka‘ba, then got out of the Ka‘ba and did the Tawaaf.

16
Adam’s Ka‘ba rituals lasted seven days, and on each day Adam repeated the same rituals.

17
After Adam and Hawwa had completed their Ka‘ba rituals, Jibreel said to them: “Allah is pleased with you. Now you can do whatever you like.”

18
Jibreel gave Adam Allah’s Book and said: “This is Allah’s Book to help you and Hawwa negotiate your way on earth.”

19
Adam looked heavenwards and said: “Thank You, O Magnanimous Lord of Hope, but it is cold on earth.”

20
Allah sent Jibreel down to earth with a paradisial ruby in the shape of a tent, which had three lanterns of paradisial gold brightening the tent with a pleasant paradisial light.

21
Jibreel said to Adam and Hawwa: “This paradisial ruby tent is your new home. Allah’s House the Ka‘ba and the paradisial ruby tent are guarded by the Raqee soldier angels to keep out Iblees and his Shayaateen who are banned from paradise, for whoever enters Allah’s House the Ka‘ba or this paradisial ruby tent gains entry to paradise. Welcome home.”

22
Adam and Hawwa said: “By the Blessing of Allah, the Merciful Lord of Forgiveness and Love,” then walked into their new home and were swept by their emotions.

SURA THIRTY THREE

The Fire

1
The following day Jibreel brought the fire, an anvil, a hammer, a pair of tongs and a bellows from Jabal Abu Qubais.

2
Jibreel put the fire in one of Adam's hands, but the fire burnt Adam's hand and Adam threw it in the sea.

3
Jibreel picked up the fire, dipped it in the sea to cool its temper, and then put it in Adam's hand, but the fire burnt Adam's hand and Adam threw it again in the sea.

4
Every time Jibreel put the fire in Adam's hand the fire burnt Adam's hand and Adam threw it in the sea.

5
The seventh time Adam threw the fire in the sea, Jibreel picked up the fire and dipped it in the sea to cool its temper, and as he was about to put it in Adam's hand, Adam said: "Why does the fire burn my hand but not yours?"

6
Jibreel said: "Because you have disobeyed Allah and I have not."

7
The eighth time Jibreel put the fire in Adam's hand, Adam threw it in the sea, Jibreel picked up the fire and dipped it in the sea seventy times to cool its temper, and then put it in Adam's hand, and the fire screamed at Adam: "You broke your promise to Allah, you disobedient and ungrateful creature. I detest you!"

8
Adam was shaken by the fire's unprovoked outburst.

9
Adam looked at Jibreel, then at the fire, and said in a subdued tone: "There is no need to be offensive. Allah has forgiven me. Ask Jibreel."

10
The fire faced Jibreel and said: "Is Adam telling the truth?"

11
Jibreel nodded and said: "Yes, Allah has forgiven Adam. Try to be kind to Adam, he is one of Allah's favourite creatures."

12
The fire said agitatingly: "Jibreel, dont try your smooth talk with me."

13
Jibreel was serious.

14
The fire crackled aggressively at Adam: "I will not forgive you."

15
Jibreel said to Adam: “The fire is useful. But since the fire doesnt like you, it will not obey you, so I will store it in wood, stone and iron. And whenever you need the fire you rub two stones together over dry wood, and the fire stored in the stones will spark out of the stones and light the fire stored in the wood.”

16
Adam said to Jibreel: “Why do I need the fire? I have done without it up till now. This fire is harsh and it stings and burns.”

17
Jibreel said: “This earthly fire is reminiscent of the fires of hell, and its harshness and stinging burns are nothing compared to those of the fires of hell. The earthly fire is to remind you of what you will suffer if you break your promise again. The earthly fire is beneficial when properly used. Handle the fire with care.”

SURA THIRTY FOUR

Survival

1
Adam and Hawwa, who had eaten nothing since their expulsion from paradise, said to Jibreel: “We are very hungry.”

2
Jibreel heard the rumbling stomachs of Adam and Hawwa and said: “Wait here.”

3
Jibreel flew to paradise and came back with a pair of big, red bulls, a pair of sheep, a pair of goats and a pair of camels.

4
Jibreel taught Adam and Hawwa to extract iron from rocks and beat the redhot iron into knives, shears, ploughs, pickaxes and stone cutting tools.

5
Mikaa’eel gave Adam and Hawwa seven grains of wheat, and each grain was as white as snow and as large as an ostrich egg.

6
The sight of the seven grains of wheat frightened Adam and Hawwa.

7
Adam and Hawwa said to Mikaa’eel: “We dont want this fruit. This is the fruit of the Testing Tree, the same fruit that got us out of paradise.”

8
Mikaa'eel said: "Since you chose to eat the fruit of the Testing Tree in Jannat Adan, the fruit of the Testing Tree will be your food and the food of your offspring on earth."

9
Jibreel taught Adam and Hawwa ploughing and sowing.

10
Adam and Hawwa ploughed the field and sowed the seven grains of wheat, and the seven grains of wheat grew instantly as tall as palm trees, with ears of wheat thirty metres long ready for harvesting.

11
Jibreel taught Adam and Hawwa wheatcutting.

12
Adam and Hawwa cut the wheat and said: "Can we eat the fruit of the Testing Tree?"

13
Jibreel said: "Not yet."

14
Jibreel taught Adam and Hawwa threshing.

15
Adam and Hawwa threshed the wheat and said: "Can we eat the threshed fruit?"

16
Jibreel said: "Not yet."

17
Jibreel got two stones and put some grains of wheat between the two stones and taught Adam and Hawwa grinding.

18
Adam and Hawwa ground the grains of wheat and said: “Can we eat the flour?”

19
Jibreel said: “Not yet.”

20
Jibreel added water to the flour and taught Adam and Hawwa kneading.

21
Adam and Hawwa kneaded the dough and said: “Can we eat the dough?”

22
Jibreel said: “Not yet.”

23
Jibreel dug a hole in the ground and lit a fire in the hole and taught Adam and Hawwa baking.

24
Adam and Hawwa baked the dough and said: “Can we eat the bread?”

25
Jibreel said: “Wait until sunset, and then you can break your fast by eating the bread.”

26
Adam and Hawwa walked up to the top of the nearby mountain to have a full view of their surroundings, and at sunset they held the bread in their hands, but the bread slipped out of their hands and tumbled down the mountain.

27
Adam and Hawwa ran after the bread and caught it.

28
Allah observed: "How impatient are these creatures."

29
Jibreel said to Adam and Hawwa: "You didnt have to do that. If you had waited a little longer the bread would have come to you."

30
Adam and Hawwa said: "We didnt know that. We are very hungry."

31
Allah observed: "How impatient are these creatures."

32
Jibreel said to Adam and Hawwa: "Now you can eat in peace."

33
Adam and Hawwa said: "By the Blessing of Allah, the Merciful Lord of Forgiveness and Love," then broke their fast by eating the bread and regained their strength.

34
Mikaa'eel brought from paradise a vine tree, a palm tree, a pomegranate tree, an apple tree, a quince tree, a pear tree, an apricot tree, a peach tree, a plum tree, a jujube tree, a mulberry tree, a carob tree, a banana tree, a lemon tree, a watermelon tree, a cucumber tree, a walnut tree, an almond tree, a pistachio tree, a hazelnut tree, a chestnut tree, a coconut tree, an oak tree, a medlar tree and a poppy tree.

35
Jibreel taught Adam and Hawwa tree planting.

36
Adam and Hawwa planted the paradisial trees, and the paradisial trees bore fruit instantly.

37
Jibreel taught Adam and Hawwa fruit picking.

38
Adam and Hawwa picked the fruit of the paradisial trees and said: "Can we eat the fruit of the paradisial trees?"

39
Jibreel said: "Yes, you can eat the fruit of the paradisial trees."

40
Adam and Hawwa said: "By the Blessing of Allah, the Merciful Lord of Forgiveness and Love," then ate the fruit and felt refreshed.

41
Jibreel taught Adam and Hawwa to shear the wool of the sheep, the goats and the camels.

42
Adam and Hawwa sheared the wool of the sheep, the goats and the camels.

43
Jibreel taught Adam and Hawwa to spin the sheared wool into threads.

44
Adam and Hawwa spun the sheared wool into threads.

45
Jibreel taught Adam and Hawwa to weave the threads into clothes.

46
Adam and Hawwa wove the threads into clothes.

47
Adam and Hawwa said: "By the Blessing of Allah, the Merciful Lord of Forgiveness and Love," then wore the clothes and felt warm.

48
Adam and Hawwa devoted their time to work and prayer, but there were times when they were so busy that they forgot to pray.

49
Allah noted Adam and Hawwa's oversight.

50
Allah sent Adam and Hawwa a hen and a white cockerel which was as big as a bull and had two crests and yellow legs.

51
Allah said to Adam and Hawwa: "When the cockerel flaps its wings it is time for you to pray."

52
Adam and Hawwa said: "Thank you, Lord, we will remember that."

53
The angels, fascinated by the way Adam and Hawwa were coping with the mountains, iron, fire, water and wind, said to Allah: "Lord, is there anything stronger than the mountains?"

54
Allah said: "Yes, iron."

55
The angels said: "Lord, is there anything stronger than iron?"

56
Allah said: "Yes, fire."

57
The angels said: "Lord, is there anything stronger than fire?"

58
Allah said: “Yes, water.”

59
The angels said: “Lord, is there anything stronger than water?”

60
Allah said: “Yes, wind.”

61
The angels said: “Lord, is there anything stronger than wind?”

62
Allah said: “Yes, Man.”

SURA THIRTY FIVE

Encounter

1
One of the Shayaateen search parties tracking down Adam and Hawwa arrived in Mecca and noticed a brilliant light emanating from the paradisial ruby tent and the Ka'ba.

2
A member of the Shayaateen search party said: "Look at those creatures of light guarding the brilliant light behind them. And look at those two strange creatures moving about, they are unlike any earthly creatures we know. They must be Adam and Hawwa. We must report this to Iblees at once."

3
The Shayaateen search party reported their finding to Iblees.

4
Iblees thought: "Adam and Hawwa must be in the Sacred Land of Mecca."

5
Iblees was on the road to Mecca.

6
The moment Iblees was in Mecca he dashed to the Ka'ba hoping to meet Adam and Hawwa and gain entry to paradise, but the Raqee soldier angels guarding the Ka'ba prevented him from entering the Ka'ba.

7
Iblees darted to the paradisial ruby tent hoping to meet Adam and Hawwa and gain entry to paradise, but the Raqee soldier angels guarding the paradisial ruby tent prevented him from entering the paradisial ruby tent.

8
Iblees waited outside the paradisial ruby tent until Adam and Hawwa came out.

9
Iblees said to Adam and Hawwa: "Salaam, you two. Glad to see you again. I am your friend Iblees. I have been worried about you for a long time, because life on this cold and inhospitable earth is unbearable without friends. But now that I am with you your problems are over. I will help you fight the cold and provide you with your favourite food and show you the stunning sights I am sure you will love. Believe me, life on earth can be just as pleasant as it was in paradise."

10
Adam shouted at Iblees: "You already got us out of paradise. What else do you want? Beat it."

11
Iblees pretended to be upset and cried, then said pointing an accusing finger at Adam: "Had it not been for you I would still be in paradise. It was on your account I got thrown out of paradise."

12
Iblees tried again and again to win the confidence of Adam and Hawwa, and when his attempts got him nowhere he thought of another plan.

13
Iblees paid a courtesy visit to the earthly animals and said to them: “Salaam, old friends. Remember me? I am your old friend the pious Iblees who shielded your noble ancestors from the genii who were hunting them to extinction. Just as I did your noble ancestors a favour, I will also do you a favour, and I expect nothing in return. It is my nature to help others and see that they come to no harm. And that is why I am here. I have come back from paradise to warn you of the new danger that will destroy you and your habitat. This danger is called Adam and Hawwa whom Allah created out of stinking earthly soil. Remember the Rimms, and how they almost exterminated you: they were also created out of stinking earthly soil. I have no doubt Adam and Hawwa will be more ruthless than the Rimms because, unlike the Rimms, Allah created them in His Own Image with His Own Hands, and are therefore more deadly than their predecessors. So I suggest you kill Adam and Hawwa now before they exterminate you.”

14
Unmoved by Iblees’s words, the earthly animals said: “We have heard about you, Iblees. Your name crops up in our ancient akhbar, akhbar poems and songs. But for all your worth, we think you are exaggerating the menace of Adam and Hawwa. We have met Adam and Hawwa many times and they were always friendly to us.”

15
Iblees, who had heard of what the eagle and the fish said about Adam and Hawwa, reinforced his argument: "You can verify what I said about Adam and Hawwa with the eagle and the fish. Dont waste time. Act now. I swear by Allah I am giving you a sincere advice. But if you stubbornly insist on being fooled by the friendliness of Adam and Hawwa, then dont say I didnt warn you."

16
The earthly animals debated Iblees's warning.

17
The dog said: "What if Iblees is telling the truth?"

18
The earthly animals said in unison: "Let us all go to Adam and Hawwa and see if they mean to harm us. And you, dog, as you are the bravest among us, you can lead us."

19
The dog said: "Let us go then."

20
Adam and Hawwa, who were on Jabal Mina, saw the earthly animals headed by the dog coming towards them menacingly.

21
Adam called Jibreel: "Jibreel, I dont like the aggressive looks on the animals' faces."

22
Jibreel responded: "Adam, when Allah's creature the dog comes to you stroke his head."

23
The dog came to Adam and Adam stroked his head, and the dog crouched peacefully at Adam's feet.

24
The earthly animals saw the dog crouching peacefully at Adam's feet and said: "Adam and Hawwa are not like what Iblees told us."

25
The earthly animal crowd broke up and went about their business.

26
Iblees was disappointed and said to himself: "Allah's earthly animals are unreliable. I will have another go at Adam and Hawwa."

27
Iblees approached Adam and Hawwa and said: "Salaam, Adam and Hawwa."

28
Jibreel said to Adam and Hawwa: "Each of you throw seven stones at Iblees, and each time you throw a stone invoke Allah's protection and make a wish."

29
Adam and Hawwa threw the prescribed stones at Iblees, invoked Allah's protection and made a wish: "Lord, help us to protect ourselves from Iblees and to return to paradise."

30
Iblees moved away from Adam and Hawwa and said to himself: "Adam and Hawwa are not as bad as they seem."

31
Iblees approached Adam and Hawwa again and said: "Why are you so touchy every time I talk to you?"

32
Jibreel said to Adam and Hawwa: "Each of you throw seven stones at Iblees, and each time you throw a stone invoke Allah's protection and make a wish."

33
Adam and Hawwa threw the prescribed stones at Iblees, invoked Allah's protection and made a wish: "Lord, help us to protect ourselves from Iblees and to return to paradise."

34
Iblees moved away from Adam and Hawwa and said to himself: "Adam and Hawwa are not as bad as they seem."

35
Iblees approached Adam and Hawwa again and said: "What is the matter with you two? Every time I talk to you, each of you throws seven stones at me. Have I done you any wrong? Tell me. As you and I are the only inhabitants of this earth, we might as well be friends and help one another. In any case, it is

I who helped you come to this place. So let us work together and turn the earth into a lasting paradise."

36
Jibreel said to Adam and Hawwa: "Each of you throw seven stones at Iblees, and each time you throw a stone invoke Allah's protection and make a wish."

37
Adam and Hawwa threw the prescribed stones at Iblees, invoked Allah's protection and made a wish: "Lord, help us to protect ourselves from Iblees and to return to paradise."

38
Iblees moved away from Adam and Hawwa in despair and said to himself: "Why should I waste my time with Adam and Hawwa? They are of no use to me, Allah can have them. I hope I will have better luck with their offspring. It is time I settled down and had a family and brought up my ten immortal children who will assist me to frustrate Allah's plans to control the earth. Sooner or later Allah will have to come to terms with the fact that the earth is my domain and it is I, Iblees, who is the absolute ruler of the earth, and whoever rules any land will be my shadow on that land and accountable to me."

39
Iblees took to the sky and stopped in midair and said to the air: "Air, if you are above me lift me up to you, if you are below me pull me down to you."

40
Iblees heard a voice booming: "Iblees, Allah is everywhere."

41
Fear shook Iblees and his teeth chattered and sparked, and out of his teethy sparks sprang his first ten immortal offspring whom he named: Thabir, A'war, Maisoot, Daasim, Zalanboor, Mudhbal, Khanzab, Haffaaq, Murra, Walhaan and Mutaqaadi.

42
Iblees withdrew with his ten immortal offspring to his Wadi Abqar retreat to bring them up and prepare them for their earthly task as agreed with Allah.

43
Jibreel said to Adam and Hawwa: "Iblees will not bother you any more."

SURA THIRTY SIX

Allah's House Bait Ma'moor

1
Allah said to Jibreel: "Move Adam and Hawwa away from the paradisial ruby tent and My House the Ka'ba. I will visit My House the Ka'ba and check the foundations of My new House Bait Ma'moor to be built on the grounds of the paradisial ruby tent, so the angels guarding My House the Ka'ba and the paradisial ruby tent and the angels visiting the earth can pray and do the Tawaaf round My House Bait Ma'moor."

2
Jibreel moved Adam to Jabal Safa and Hawwa to Jabal Marwa, then lifted the paradisial ruby tent heavenwards.

3
Adam said to Jibreel: "Why have you separated me from Hawwa and brought me here? Is Allah angry with me?"

4
Jibreel said to Adam: "Allah is not angry with you. It is Allah's Will you should be separated from Hawwa, and no one questions Allah's Will."

5
Adam missed Hawwa.

6
Adam descended from Jabal Safa and was lost in the wadi.

7
Adam looked for Jabal Marwa but Jabal Marwa was nowhere in sight.

8
The fear of being alone again haunted Adam.

9
Adam called Hawwa again and again but got no response.

10
All at once Adam spotted Jabal Marwa and rushed up the mountain and was glad to be with Hawwa.

11
Adam and Hawwa were swept by their emotions.

12
Jibreel said to Adam: "Now that you have seen Hawwa it is time you got back to Jabal Safa."

13
Adam said: "But I have only just arrived and not without an effort."

14
Jibreel said: "It is time you got back to Jabal Safa. You can visit Hawwa tomorrow."

15
Adam went back to Jabal Safa reluctantly.

16
Adam visited Hawwa a second time.

17
Adam visited Hawwa a third time.

18
Adam and Hawwa turned their gaze towards the grounds of their paradisial ruby tent and saw Allah's newly built House Bait Ma'moor being completed.

19
Jibreel said to Adam: "It is time you got back to Jabal Safa."

20
Adam went back to Jabal Safa reluctantly.

21
Adam prayed: "Lord, I miss being with Hawwa. Lord, can we go back to our paradisial ruby tent?"

22
Allah said to Jibreel: "Tell Adam and Hawwa they can go back to their paradisial ruby tent."

23
Jibreel said to Adam: "Allah's House Bait Ma'moor is ready. Go and collect Hawwa and return to your paradisial ruby tent standing next to Allah's House Bait Ma'moor."

24
Adam ran down Jabal Safa, through the wadi, up Jabal Marwa and was glad to be with Hawwa.

25
Adam said to Hawwa: “We can go home now.”

26
In Mecca Adam and Hawwa first prayed and did the Tawaaf round Bait Ma‘moor, then prayed and did the Tawaaf round the Ka‘ba, and then ambled happily to their paradisial ruby tent and were swept by their emotions.

SURA THIRTY SEVEN

The Bay

1
Allah thought: "It is time Adam and Hawwa explored the earth."

2
Allah ordered the South Wind: "South Wind, stop there."

3
The South Wind stopped.

4
Allah told Jibreel: "Get Me a handful of South Wind."

5
Jibreel brought a handful of South Wind to Allah.

6
And out of the handful of South Wind Allah created a bay.

7
Allah presented Adam with the heavenly riding creature Buraaq and the newly created bay and said: "Adam, choose one of the two riding creatures."

8
Adam looked at the two riding creatures, then pointed at the bay and said: "Lord, I will have this one because it is the finest of the two and it reminds me of the winged mare on which I toured the seven paradises."

9
And out of the same handful of South Wind Allah created another bay and gave it to Hawwa.

10
Allah said to Adam and Hawwa: "Now you can go and explore the earth."

11
Adam and Hawwa went to the Ka'ba and prayed and did the Tawaaf, then mounted the bays and said: "By the Blessing of Allah, the Merciful Lord of Forgiveness and Love," and then embarked on their journey around the earth.

12
Adam and Hawwa travelled all over the earth and were eyethrilled by the everchanging scenery of each region they visited, and made friends with all the earthly creatures they met.

13
When Adam and Hawwa were in Sri Lanka, Adam pointed at Jabal Raahoon and said: "That is the mountain where I was mountainbound for the first hundred years of my earthly life."

14
Hawwa was exhilarated: "Let us go up the mountain and see if there are any traces of your sojourn there."

15
Adam was excited: "Come on then."

16
Adam and Hawwa rushed to the top of the mountain and saw footmarks.

17
Hawwa said: "These must be your footmarks."

18
All at once Adam was gripped by sadness and said: "Yes, they are my footmarks."

19
Adam looked heavenwards and remembered his ordeal and said: "From here I heard the comforting prayers of the heavenly angels, but now, alas, I can hear nothing. Hawwa, I miss paradise, but most of all I miss the Sacred Land of Mecca, Allah's House the Ka'ba, the paradisial Stone of Consolation, Jabal Safa, Jabal Marwa, Jabal Arafa and Jabal Mina, that are our only link with paradise."

20
Hawwa consoled Adam: "Dont be depressed, all is not lost, paradise is still within our grasp. Let us go back to the Sacred Land of Mecca and visit Allah's House the Ka'ba and live our lives as we promised Allah."

21
Adam was consoled by Hawwa's comforting words and said: "You are right. Let us go back to the Sacred Land of Mecca."

22
Adam and Hawwa were back in Mecca exactly one year since the day of their departure from Mecca, and on their arrival they

went straight to the Ka'ba and prayed and did the Tawaaf and kissed the paradisial Stone of Consolation, then walked to Jabal Safa, Jabal Marwa and Jabal Arafa and recalled nostalgically the day of their reunion on earth, then walked to Jabal Mina and each of them threw seven stones three times at the spot where Iblees tried to break their resolve and made the wish of returning to paradise, then walked back to the Ka'ba and prayed and did the Tawaaf and then ambled happily to their paradisial ruby tent.

23
Before sleeping Adam said: "This time I feel our visit to Allah's House the Ka'ba is different from our previous visits. I feel closer to Allah in a way I have never felt before."

24
Hawwa said: "I feel the same."

25
Adam and Hawwa fell asleep overwhelmed by a feeling of peace.

26
In the morning Adam and Hawwa decided to make their return to Mecca and their visit to the Ka'ba, Jabal Safa, Jabal Marwa, Jabal Arafa and the throwing of the stones on Jabal Mina an annual seven day Hajj event to confirm their faith in Allah's promise.

SURA THIRTY EIGHT

The Children

1
Hawwa was pregnant, but on the eighth month of her pregnancy she had a miscarriage.

2
Hawwa was pregnant again, but she was no more fortunate in this pregnancy than in her previous one.

3
The third time Hawwa was pregnant she and Adam were afraid of another miscarriage.

4
Adam and Hawwa prayed: "Lord, if we could only have a child like other earthly creatures."

5
Iblees was told of the wish of Adam and Hawwa by his soldier Shaayaateen who were shadowing Adam and Hawwa and said to himself: "Now is the time to strike."

6
Iblees approached Hawwa and said: "Do you want the baby in your womb to survive?"

7
Hawwa said: "Yes."

8
Iblees said: “Allah has sent me to help you. It is Allah’s Will that when your baby is born you name the baby Abdulhaarith if he is a boy or Amatulhaarith if she is a girl.”

9
Adam and Hawwa were in no mood to question the motives of Iblees, and when Hawwa gave birth to a baby boy he was named Abdulhaarith.

10
An angel visited Adam and Hawwa and said: “Why did you name your son Abdulhaarith?”

11
Adam and Hawwa said: “We named our son Abdulhaarith so he may live.”

12
The angel said: “You could have named your son Abdullah, or Abdurrahmaan or Abdurraheem. Have you forgotten that Haarith was Iblees’s original name?”

13
Adam said: “Hawwa and I were so worried we might lose the boy that we forgot that Haarith was Iblees’s original name. We dont want this baby, get rid of him.”

14
Abdulhaarith died instantly.

15
Adam and Hawwa, fearful of Allah's retribution, prayed: "Forgive us, O Lord of All Creation."

16
Allah Who was Merciful and Forgiving considered the desperate state of Adam and Hawwa and forgave them.

17
Iblees was disappointed by the sudden death of Abdulhaarith and said to himself: "Allah is determined not to let me spoil His plans for Adam and Hawwa."

18
Allah thought: "It is time Adam and Hawwa had children."

19
Hawwa became pregnant.

20
Adam and Hawwa prayed anxiously: "Lord, help us to have this baby."

21
Allah said to Adam and Hawwa: "Have no fear. You will have many children."

22
Adam and Hawwa had many children, and all the children were born as twins, a boy and a girl.

23
The first children to be born were Qaabeel and his twin sister followed five years later by Haabeel and his twin sister.

24
Qaabeel's twin sister was beautiful and Haabeel's twin sister was ugly.

25
When Haabeel was twenty he said to Adam: "Father, I want to marry Qaabeel's twin sister, and Qaabeel can marry my twin sister."

26
Adam agreed to Haabeel's request, but not Qaabeel.

27
Qaabeel protested: "Father, my twin sister is more beautiful than Haabeel's twin sister, and since I knew my twin sister before Haabeel and I am five years older than him, I am more entitled to marry her than him."

28
Adam said: "Qaabeel, it is Allah's Will that no one should marry his twin sister."

29
Qaabeel said: "Father, Haabeel will not marry my twin sister. It is I who will marry my twin sister."

30
Adam was at a loss.

31
Allah said to Adam: “If you have a problem you cannot resolve, go to My House the Ka‘ba and tell Me about your problem and I will solve it for you.”

32
Adam followed Allah’s advice, but before going to the Ka‘ba he said to the sky: “Could you look after Haabeel while I am away?”

33
But the sky said: “No, I cannot look after Haabeel while you are away.”

34
Adam turned to the mountains and said: “Could you look after Haabeel while I am away?”

35
But the mountains said: “No, we cannot look after Haabeel while you are away.”

36
Adam turned to the trees and said: “Could you look after Haabeel while I am away?”

37
But the trees said: “No, we cannot look after Haabeel while you are away.”

38
Adam turned to the earth and said: “Could you look after Haabeel while I am away?”

39
But the earth said: "No, I cannot look after Haabeel while you are away."

40
Adam then turned to Qaabeel and said: "Could you look after your brother Haabeel while I am away?"

41
Qaabeel said: "Yes, father, I will look after my brother Haabeel while you are away."

42
Adam withdrew to the Ka'ba and said: "Lord, I am in a dilemma. Haabeel wants to marry Qaabeel's twin sister, which is what Your prescribed in Your Divine Book, but Qaabeel insists on marrying her himself. There is nothing I can do to enforce Your Word."

43
Allah said: "You have done the right thing in coming to Me. Let Qaabeel and Haabeel decide what to do. But you can tell them that since I am their Lord and Creator, I am the One Whose Judgement is final. Tell them to make an offering to Me on Jabal Mina, and the one whose offering I accept will marry the twin sister of the other. And if they dont go along with My Will they will be punished."

44
Adam told Qaabeel and Haabeel of Allah's Will.

45
Qaabeel and Haabeel agreed to follow Allah's Will.

46
Qaabeel was a farmer, and he gathered a batch of ears of wheat, and in the batch he spotted a wholesome ear of wheat and said to himself: "This wholesome ear of wheat is for me."

47
Qaabeel picked the wholesome ear of wheat and ate it.

48
Qaabeel looked at the rest of the ears of wheat and said to himself: "These ears of wheat are good enough for Allah."

49
Haabeel was a shepherd, and he chose a white lamb he reared as a pet called Jareer and said to himself: "I am going to offer Allah my treasured lamb Jareer."

50
Allah observed Haabeel and Qaabeel and thought: "Haabeel is unlike Qaabeel."

51
Adam accompanied Qaabeel and Haabeel to the top of Jabal Mina where Qaabeel and Haabeel laid out their offerings.

52
Adam, Qaabeel and Haabeel sat and focused on the offerings.

53
A white, heatless, smokeless fire descended from the first heaven Birqi and hovered above Haabeel's lamb and swallowed it, then withdrew to the first heaven Birqi, leaving Qaabeel's offering untouched.

54
Qaabeel was a mass of envy and resentment.

55
Adam discerned from Allah's rejection of Qaabeel's offering that Allah was displeased with Qaabeel, and was intimating that Haabeel should be appointed as his successor as Allah's Caliph on earth.

56
Adam said to Qaabeel: "Since Allah has accepted Haabeel's offering, it is Allah's Will that Haabeel should marry your twin sister and be my successor as Allah's Caliph on earth."

57
Qaabeel said: "Father, your love for Haabeel compelled you to persuade Allah to accept Haabeel's offering and to be your successor as Allah's Caliph on earth. Haabeel can have the Caliphate but he will not marry my twin sister."

58
Adam reminded Qaabeel of Allah's Will, then left the two brothers to thrash it out.

59
Haabeel said to Qaabeel: "What are you fuming about? Allah has accepted my offering because He knows I believe in Him."

60
Qaabeel said: "I believe in Allah as much as you do."

61
Haabeel said: “If you believe in Allah, then comply with Allah’s Will.”

62
Qaabeel said: “You will not marry my twin sister even if Allah wills it.”

63
Haabeel said: “It is not up to you to decide who should marry whom. Allah, Our Lord and Creator, will see to it I marry your twin sister.”

64
Qaabeel said: “I am not through with you. You will not get away with it.”

65
Haabeel said: “I have done you no wrong, why should you threaten me? If you cause me any harm I will not retaliate, Allah will punish you.”

66
Once Qaabeel saw Haabeel asleep in the field with his head resting on a stone and wondered how to get rid of him.

67
Iblees, who was always close to hand at the opportune moment, assumed the form of a bird and landed near Qaabeel and said: “Qaabeel, do you want to get rid of Haabeel so he will not bother you any more?”

68
Qaabeel said: “Yes, but I dont know how.”

69
Iblees said: “Watch me.”

70
Iblees chased and clawed a passing bird and put its head on a stone and smashed it with another stone, and said: “Do as I did. Get a stone and hit Haabeel hard on the head. I am not pushing you to do something against your will. But I must tell you that if you dont get rid of Haabeel, he will one day have children who will boast over your children and say ‘We are the children of Haabeel whose offering was accepted by Allah, and you are the children of Qaabeel whose offering was rejected by Allah’. So get rid of Haabeel now and spare your children an unnecessary humiliation.”

71
Qaabeel grabbed a stone and hit Haabeel hard on the head, smashing his head and killing him.

72
After Qaabeel’s anger had abated Qaabeel noticed Haabeel’s head bleeding and did not understand what he had done.

73
Qaabeel called his brother: “Haabeel!”

74
But Haabeel was silent.

75
Qaabeel called again: “Haabeel! Haabeel! Haabeel!”

76
But Haabeel was silent.

77
Qaabeel shook his brother and called again: “Haabeel! Haabeel! Talk to me Haabeel!”

78
But Haabeel was still silent.

79
Qaabeel panicked and said to Iblees: “Why is Haabeel not speaking to me?”

80
Iblees said: “Haabeel is not speaking to you because he is dead.”

81
Qaabeel said: “What have I done?”

82
Iblees said: “You have got rid of Haabeel.”

83
Qaabeel said: “But Haabeel is here, only he wouldnt speak to me.”

84
Iblees said: “Yes, Haabeel is here, but he will not speak to you because you have smashed his life out of him. Have a good look at Haabeel, this is the last time you see him.”

85
Qaabeel said: “What shall I do?”

86
Iblees said: “Nothing.”

87
Qaabeel said: “What if my father asks about Haabeel?”

88
Iblees said: “Just say you dont know where Haabeel is.”

89
Qaabeel said: “What if my father insists on knowing where Haabeel is?”

90
Iblees said: “Stop worrying.”

91
Qaabeel said: “Something is stinging me.”

92
Iblees said: “Stop complaining. You are imagining things.”

93
Iblees said to himself: “Good. My soldier Shayaateen are at work, poking Qaabeel with their plague spears.”

94
Qaabeel said: “Haabeel is dead.”

95
Iblees said: “Calm down.”

96
Qaabeel said: “What am I going to say to my father?”

97
Iblees said: “Say to your father you had been working all day in the field, and as Haabeel is a shepherd he could be anywhere with his flock.”

98
Qaabeel said to himself: “Maybe my father will believe me when I tell him Haabeel could be anywhere with his flock.”

99
Iblees grinned and said to himself: “Qaabeel will not be as difficult as Adam and Hawwa. I think he is an easy catch.”

100
While Qaabeel was talking to Iblees, Allah sent a crow which alighted by a dead crow not far from Qaabeel.

101
The crow carked and drew Qaabeel’s attention.

102
The crow dug a hole in the ground with its beak and claws and shoved the dead crow in the hole, then levelled the hole with the dugout soil.

103
Qaabeel was amazed by the activity of the crow and said to himself: "Damn me! What has become of me that I should learn from a crow what to do with Haabeel's body?"

104
Qaabeel dug a deep hole in the ground and pushed Haabeel's body in the hole and levelled the hole with the dugout soil, and said to himself: "No one will know where Haabeel is. It is getting late, I had better get home otherwise my mother and father will worry about me."

105
As Qaabeel was leaving, an owl emerged from Haabeel's grave and perched on the grave screeching incessantly: "Give me a drink! Give me a drink!"

106
Qaabeel stopped and gazed at the owl perched on Haabeel's grave and mumbled: "I wonder what the owl means by 'Give me a drink'."

107
Iblees volunteered: "When you smashed Haabeel's head with the stone, the soul of Haabeel came out of his head as blood that turned into the screeching owl perched on his grave, and the owl will go on with its intolerable screeching until Haabeel is avenged, and once he is avenged, the owl will melt away and he will have peace. But if Haabeel had died of natural causes, his soul would have come out of his head as an owl and commuted between him and his family and reported family news to him for a hundred years. The soul owl of a dead man is called Sada and the soul owl of a dead woman is called Haama."

108
Qaabeel said: "What is avenge?"

109
Iblees said: "To kill the killer of the killed. And since you killed Haabeel, that is you smashed his life out of him, the owl will go on screeching 'Give me a drink' until you are killed."

110
Qaabeel paused, then said to himself: "I have nothing to fear. There is only me and my two sisters, and they wouldnt dare to touch me because I am stronger than they are. As for my mother and father, they wouldnt kill me because I am the only son left."

111
Qaabeel stared at the owl perched on Haabeel's grave for a long while, then said: "You can screech as much as you like. I am going home now."

112
Iblees said: "Qaabeel, where are you off to?"

113
Qaabeel said: "I am going home."

114
Iblees grinned.

115
Iblees rushed to Hawwa who was sitting outside the paradisial ruby tent and said: "Hawwa, I have bad news for you."

116
Hawwa said: "Go away, Iblees, you bring nothing but disaster. I am not interested in what you want to tell me. Beat it."

117
Iblees said: "Dont be so prickly, woman."

118
Hawwa said: "Dont call me woman. My name is Hawwa, and I am a mother."

119
Iblees said: "All right, mother Hawwa. I am going, but dont say I didnt try to tell you about your son Haabeel."

120
Hawwa said: "What of Haabeel?"

121
Iblees said: "Qaabeel has killed Haabeel."

122
Hawwa said: "What is killing?"

123
Iblees said: "One who doesnt eat nor drink nor move."

124
Hawwa said: "That is death."

125
Iblees said: "That is correct. Haabeel is dead, Qaabeel killed him."

126
Hawwa screamed.

127
Adam heard the scream and ran to Hawwa and said: "Why did you scream?"

128
But Hawwa was silent.

129
Adam asked Hawwa again and again: "Why did you scream?"

130
But Hawwa was silent.

131
The silence of Hawwa and the tense atmosphere almost cracked the nerves of Adam who, after his expulsion from paradise, was always afraid of doing anything that might displease Allah and ultimately affect his chances of returning with Hawwa to paradise.

132
Adam fixed his eyes on Hawwa and said in a desperate tone: "Is there anyone who can tell me what is wrong?"

133
Iblees, who discreetly stayed out of the way while Adam was addressing Hawwa, intruded: "I can tell you what is wrong."

134
Adam recognised the voice of Iblees and said: “Iblees, it is you again. Mind your own business. Push off.”

135
Adam paused, then called frantically: “Qaabeel! Haabeel! Qaabeel! Haabeel! Where are you? Answer me.”

136
Iblees said gravely: “Haabeel is dead, Qaabeel killed him, that is Haabeel doesnt eat nor drink nor move.”

137
Adam said: “You are out of your mind. Qaabeel wouldnt do such a thing. You are here to stir up trouble in my family. Scram.”

138
Iblees said indifferently: “If you doubt what I said about Qaabeel and Haabeel why didnt they respond to your call?”

139
Adam looked around him and saw the earth, the trees, the mountains and the wadis changing colour and turning grey, and the grey trees growing thorns, and the animals running away from him snarling nervously, no longer able to communicate with one another; and from that day the grey trees bore only seasonal fruit.

140
Adam looked at the sky, and the sky was riddled with shooting stars.

141
Iblees volunteered: “Do you know why the earth, the trees, the mountains and the wadis have changed colour and turned grey? And why the grey trees have grown thorns? And why the animals ran away from you snarling nervously and no longer able to communicate with one another?”

142
Adam said: “No, I dont know why.”

143
Iblees said: “Do you know why the sky is riddled with shooting stars?”

144
Adam said: “No, I dont know why.”

145
Iblees said: “The earth, the trees, the mountains and the wadis have changed colour and turned grey, and the grey trees have grown thorns, and the animals have run away from you snarling nervously and no longer able to communicate with one another in anger over the killing of Haabeel by Qaabeel. The shooting stars portend either the birth of a son or the death of a Caliph or, as you may recall, Allah’s order to the Najm angels to shoot me and the genii out of the sky if any of us ventured into the sky and eavesdropped on Him and His angels. But since the birth of a son is not likely at this stage because Hawwa is not pregnant, and since I am here talking to you and all the genii are grounded, the shooting stars can only refer to one thing: the death of a Caliph. As Haabeel is your successor as Caliph, then the shooting stars indicate the death of Haabeel.”

146
Adam said: "You are very good with words."

147
Iblees said: "Why are you suspicious of everything I say?"

148
Adam said: "Ask yourself."

149
Iblees said: "I am puzzled by the way you love your children. I tell you your son Qaabeel has killed your other son Haabeel, and all you do is argue with me as though nothing has happened."

150
Adam said: "You have yourself to blame. You lied to me and Hawwa once and you could do it again. Run along and leave us in peace."

151
Iblees said: "You shouldnt blame me. Blame Allah for not being straight with you about the Testing Tree. Had you eaten the whole fruit I gave you, you would still be in paradise."

152
Adam said: "Fade away."

153
Iblees tailed off: "Adam, you are as rude and as rough and as edgy as the earth."

154
Iblees walked away with a camouflaged grin.

155
Adam said to himself as he watched Iblees walking away: “Good riddance.”

156
Adam, exhausted by his encounter with Iblees, sat beside Hawwa and wondered whether having children was a good thing.

157
Hawwa broke her silence: “Adam, what if Iblees is for once telling the truth about Qaabeel killing Haabeel?”

158
Adam said: “Iblees is Iblees, and Allah told us to avoid him and not to believe a word he says. Look what happened to us the last time I believed him.”

159
Hawwa said: “I still think you should go and check if Iblees is telling the truth instead of dismissing him and sulking beside me.”

160
Adam said: “I might as well go and check Iblees’s improbably story of Qaabeel killing Haabeel, otherwise you will not leave me in peace.”

161
Hawwa said: "Just as we did something against Allah's Will in paradise, Qaabeel might have done the same thing."

162
Adam said: "But Allah is Merciful and Forgiving, and He forgave us, and He might forgive Qaabeel, that is if Qaabeel has done anything wrong."

163
Adam got up, hugged and kissed Hawwa and said: "You have nothing to worry about, my dear. Everything will be all right."

164
Adam led Hawwa inside the paradisial ruby tent and said: "You rest in here while I go and bring Qaabeel and Haabeel home."

165
As Adam was about to leave, he and Hawwa heard footsteps at the threshold of the paradisial ruby tent.

166
Hawwa recognised the footsteps and yelled: "Qaabeel, stop there, and dont enter our paradisial ruby tent."

167
Qaabeel stopped.

168
Hawwa said: "Qaabeel, where is Haabeel?"

169
Qaabeel said: “Mother, what do you mean where is Haabeel? Has anything happened to Haabeel?”

170
Hawwa said to Adam: “You had better ask Qaabeel where is Haabeel.”

171
Adam said: “Calm down, dear. Leave it to me. Tell me, Qaabeel, where is Haabeel?”

172
Qaabeel said: “Father, how would I know where Haabeel is. He could be anywhere with his flock.”

173
Hawwa said to Adam: “Qaabeel is lying. Haabeel is dead and Qaabeel killed him.”

174
Qaabeel said to Adam: “My mother is raving about nothing.”

175
Hawwa said to Qaabeel: “I know you killed Haabeel and where you buried him.”

176
Adam said to Qaabeel: “Is it true you killed Haabeel?”

177
Qaabeel panicked and confessed his act.

178
Adam said: "What? You killed Haabeel?"

179
Qaabeel said: "What of it if Haabeel is not with us any more? I am here and I am also your son."

180
Adam said: "You killed Haabeel?"

181
Qaabeel said: "Yes I did kill Haabeel, but you forced me to do it. It was your excessive love for Haabeel and your coldness towards me that drove me to do what I did. If you had been fair to both of us, nothing of the kind would have happened and Haabeel would still be with us."

182
Adam said: "I loved you both in the same way."

183
Qaabeel said: "So you say."

184
Adam said: "Ask your mother."

185
Qaabeel said: "Leave my mother out of it."

186
Adam said: "What has come over you?"

187
Qaabeel said: "You wanted Haabeel to marry my twin sister."

188
Adam said: "That is not true. It was Allah's Will that Haabeel should marry your twin sister. You saw for yourself Allah's fire choosing Haabeel's offering on Jabal Mina."

189
Qaabeel said: "Allah did what you wished Him to do. Admit it, father, it was your unfairness that killed my brother, not me."

190
Adam said: "Was it Iblees who urged you to kill your brother?"

191
Qaabeel said: "It is always Iblees who gets the blame for your wrongdoing. You got yourself thrown out of paradise and blamed Iblees for it. But you could not fool Allah, and you cannot fool me."

192
Adam swelled into a nimbus cloud of fury and thundered: "Qaabeel, you have committed an unforgivable crime. Allah will punish you for it. Leave the Sacred Land of Mecca and never come back. Get out of my sight. May you live in fear and never have peace, and I hope you will be killed in the same way you killed your brother."

193
Qaabeel restrained himself, grabbed his twin sister's hand and walked away southwards to Aden.

194
Iblees trailed behind Qaabeel to Aden, and at the opportune moment approached Qaabeel and said: "Do you know why Allah accepted Haabeel's offering and not yours?"

195
Qaabeel said: "Because my father loved Haabeel and prayed for him."

196
Iblees said: "The reason is that Haabeel worshipped the fire and you didnt, and Allah is all fire. Was it not the fire that swallowed Haabeel's offering?"

197
Qaabeel said: "Yes, it was the fire that swallowed Haabeel's offering."

198
Iblees said: "Why not light a fire and worship it and build a temple to protect it so as to win Allah's favour?"

199
Qaabeel said: "Do you think Allah will like it?"

200
Iblees said: "Of course, Allah will like it. After all, Allah will be in His element."

201
Qaabeel said: "I will do that."

202
Iblees said: “I will show you how to light the Fire of Allah.”

203
Under Iblees’s instructions Qaabeel built a temple and lit a fire in the temple and started worshipping it as the Fire of Allah.

204
Iblees taught Qaabeel and his twin sister the fire rituals and married them before the Fire of Allah.

205
Qaabeel and his twin sister settled down and had many children.

206
As Qaabeel watched his children growing he confided in Iblees more than once: “One day my mother and father will die and I will go back with my wife and children to the Sacred Land of Mecca and establish the worship of the Fire of Allah in His House the Ka‘ba.”

207
Iblees grinned and said to himself: “Qaabeel’s return to the Sacred Land of Mecca will mark the end of Allah’s role on earth.”

SURA THIRTY NINE

The Promise

1
Adam and Hawwa were devastated by the death of Haabeel and cried for forty days, and during those forty days everything they ate or drank tasted bitter, and all around them was dismal grey.

2
Adam and Hawwa mourned Haabeel for one year, and decided not to have any more children, but on the last day of that year Adam heard a voice: "Salaam, Adam. May you live long and have many children."

3
Adam smiled for the first time since the death of Haabeel, and before long, he and Hawwa came round to the idea of having more children to compensate for the loss of Haabeel.

4
Adam and Hawwa prayed: "Lord, help us to have another son who will not let us down like Qaabeel."

5
Allah said: "You will have another son as a gift from Me, and you will call him Hibatullah, whose name and looks will remind you of Haabeel, and Hibatullah will be as kind and obedient as Haabeel, and will be My Caliph on earth after you, Adam."

6
Hawwa was pregnant and gave birth to twins, a boy and a girl, and named the boy Hibatullah.

7
Adam and Hawwa were very happy with Hibatullah, and in time they forgot Haabeel and their tragic experience.

8
After Hibatullah, Hawwa became pregnant again and again and had many twins, and they all lived to a ripe old age, and among the boys she had were Ubaad, Baaligh, Hayyaan, Hadhar, Saalih, Abdullah, Abdurrahmaan, Abdurraheem and Baariq.

9
Adam and Hawwa loved all their children, but Hibatullah was their favourite.

10
Once Adam remembered Haabeel and gathered his children and said to Hibatullah: "Hibatullah, it is Allah's Will that when I die you succeed me as Allah's Caliph on earth. Obey Allah and look after your brothers and sisters and their children, but never mix with Qaabeel and his family nor marry from them, nor let them come anywhere near Allah's House the Ka'ba. I have carved a box in which I store Allah's Book. When I die I will leave you Allah's Book with the box and this white silkspread which has the printed faces of those who will rule the earth from now to the end of time. I will also leave you a few hairs from my beard, which will help you overcome your enemies. And when these hairs turn white it is time for you to die. Treasure the box, the beard hairs and the white silkspread and follow Allah's Book."

11
Adam paused, then said to all his children: "Always listen to your brother Hibatullah and obey him for, as he will be Allah's Caliph on earth, by obeying him you will be obeying Allah."

12
Adam's children said: "We will listen to and obey our eldest brother Hibatullah as you wish."

13
Adam and Hawwa lived for a thousand happy years with their children.

14
On the last day of his earthly life Adam was working in the field and Allah said to him: "Adam, today is the last day of your earthly life. Today the angel of death Azraa'eel will come and terminate your earthly life."

15
Adam said: "Lord, what is death?"

16
Allah said: "Death is the fulfilment of My Promise to the earth. When Azraa'eel brought Me a handful of soil out of which I created you, I promised the earth to give her back the handful of soil taken from her. When you or any of your offspring die you will be buried in a grave in the earth, and your bodies will turn into soil so the earth can recover what she had lost. The grave will be the Bait Haqq in which you and your offspring will be revived and judged, and you will all remain in the Bait Haqq until I order Israafeel to blow the Soor at the end of time. The graves of those who obey Me will be transformed into

miniparadises run by the judge angels Mubashshir and Basheer, and the graves of those who disobey Me will be transformed into minihells run by the judge angels Munkar and Nakeer."

17
Adam remembered his paradisial life and felt like having paradisial fruit, and said to Hibatullah who was working with him in the field: "I wish I could have some paradisial fruit. Go and find me some."

18
Hibatullah said: "Yes, father."

19
While Hibatullah was looking for paradisial fruit, he met Jibreel who said: "What are you doing, Hibatullah?"

20
Hibatullah said: "I am looking for paradisial fruit for my father."

21
Jibreel said: "You dont have to look for paradisial fruit any more, your father is dead."

22
Hibatullah said: "But my father was all right when I left him."

23
Jibreel said: "Your father died soon after you left him."

24
No sooner had Hibatullah left Adam than Azraa'eel landed infront of Adam in the form of a white sheep with wings blocking the horizons.

25
Adam fainted at the sight of Azraa'eel.

26
The angels sprinkled the water of life on Adam's face, and Adam regained consciousness.

27
Azraa'eel gave Adam the drink of death and said: "I am Azraa'eel, the angel of death. I have come to terminate your earthly life. Drink this cup to release your soul from your body of earthly soil."

28
Adam drank the drink of death and died.

29
The moment Adam died the sun eclipsed in mourning, and the earthly animals wept.

30
Hawwa, who was in the paradisial ruby tent and unaware of what had happened, heard the earthly animals weeping and got out of the paradisial ruby tent, and the earthly animals told her: "Hawwa, Adam is dead."

31
Hawwa was stunned, and for an instant stood motionless, then broke into sobs and wailing fits, beating her face and chest.

32
The earthly animals led Hawwa to Adam's corpse.

33
Hawwa lifted Adam and carried him in her arms to the paradisial ruby tent.

34
The earthly animals followed Hawwa and waited outside the paradisial ruby tent.

35
Jibreel taught Hawwa and Hibatullah the burial rites in the paradisial ruby tent.

36
Hawwa washed Adam's body and wrapped it in three shrouds which Jibreel brought from paradise and, together with her children, prayed for Adam, then carried him in her arms to the Ka'ba and laid him on the floor of the Ka'ba.

37
Hawwa and her children prayed and did the Tawaaf, then Hawwa carried Adam in her arms to the Kanz Cave on Jabal Abu Qubais, and prayed for him with her children and recounted his good qualities, and before burying him they said: "May Allah welcome Adam with Forgiveness and Love."

38
Hawwa stayed by Adam's grave for forty days without eating, then fell ill and died brokenhearted.

39
Hawwa's body was moved to the paradisial ruby tent, and in the paradisial ruby tent Hibatullah instructed his sister Fahwaa'eel, Hawwa's eldest daughter who looked like her, to wash and wrap Hawwa's body in three shrouds which Jibreel brought from paradise, then Hibatullah and his brothers and sisters prayed for Hawwa and carried her on a pall to the Ka'ba and laid her on the floor of the Ka'ba.

40
Hibatullah and his brothers and sisters prayed and did the Tawaaf, then carried Hawwa to Adam's burial cave and before burying her they said: "May Allah welcome Hawwa with Forgiveness and Love," and buried her alongside Adam, her head beside Adam's head and her legs next to Adam's legs.

41
Hibatullah and his brothers and sisters watched Jibreel lifting the paradisial ruby tent heavenwards.

42
Allah said to Jibreel: "Go down to earth and get Adam and Hawwa and meet Me in Jannat Adan."

43
Jibreel went down to the grave of Adam and Hawwa and conveyed Allah's Will to Mubashshir and Basheer, then returned with Adam and Hawwa to paradise.

44
Jibreel stopped at the paradisial Tawba gate so Adam and Hawwa could perform the purification ritual before entering paradise.

45
At the entrance of the paradisial Tawba gate were the Spring of Purification and the Spring of Eternal Youth, which bubbled out of the roots of the tree standing by the gate from the inside.

46
Jibreel filled two gold cups with water from the Spring of Purification and gave them to Adam and Hawwa and said: "Drink this."

47
Adam and Hawwa said: "By the Blessing of Allah, the Merciful Lord of Forgiveness and Love," then drank the water of Purification, which cleared their system of all earthly traces.

48
Jibreel filled another two gold cups with water from the Spring of Eternal Youth and gave them to Adam and Hawwa and said: "Drink this."

49
Adam and Hawwa said: "By the Blessing of Allah, the Merciful Lord of Forgiveness and Love," then drank the water of Eternal Youth, and their bodies regained their youth and their youthful vigour.

50
At the end of the purification ritual, Ridwaan greeted Adam and Hawwa: “Salaam, and welcome back to paradise. Lucky are those who return to paradise.”

51
Adam and Hawwa greeted Ridwaan: “Salaam, Ridwaan. It is good to be back in paradise.”

52
Jibreel and Adam and Hawwa were beamed to Allah in Jannat Adan.

53
Allah said to Adam and Hawwa: “Since both of you have kept your word, I have brought you back to life and to paradise as promised. Now you can go anywhere in paradise and eat whatever you like. And should you feel nostalgic for any period of your earthly life, you can go and sit under the Tooba Tree and recall any period of your earthly life, or any earthly period you fancy, and Naseem will sense your wish and waft a gentle breeze to stir the branches above you, and the desired period will come to life and you can relive that period for as long as you like.”

54
Allah walked with Adam and Hawwa to Dar Hayaat.

55
Allah said to Adam and Hawwa: “Enter your home in peace.”

56
Adam and Hawwa said: “By the Blessing of Allah, the Merciful Lord of Forgiveness and Love,” then entered their home Dar Hayaat.

SURA FORTY

The Death of Qaabeel

1
Iblees informed Qaabeel of the death of Adam and Hawwa and urged him: "Now is the time to go to the Sacred Land of Mecca and claim your right to the Caliphate, the Divine Book, your father's beard hairs and the silkspread with the printed faces. You are, after all, Adam's firstborn son."

2
Qaabeel said: "Do you think Hibatullah will be as understanding as you are?"

3
Iblees said: "Your little brother Hibatullah will have no choice."

4
Qaabeel said: "When I am Caliph I will institute the worship of the Fire of Allah throughout the Sacred Land of Mecca, and Allah's House the Ka'ba will be the centre of Fire Worship. Then Allah will forgive me and I will be as close to Him as my father was."

5
Iblees said: "Dont worry about Allah's forgiveness. Allah will forgive you if you introduce the worship of His Fire to His House the Ka'ba. And if you throw in a few extra prayers I am certain that Allah, the Merciful Lord of Forgiveness and Love, will be more than pleased to forgive you."

6
Qaabeel said: “We must leave for the Sacred Land of Mecca as soon as possible.”

7
Iblees said: “Be prepared for the worst in case Hibatullah is not as receptive as you would expect. Hibatullah might well be as strongheaded as Haabeel.”

8
Qaabeel said: “Your presence is reassuring. I dont know what I would have done without you.”

9
Iblees said: “I am always happy to be of help.”

10
Qaabeel said: “You have been more than helpful to me.”

11
Iblees said: “I have done nothing out of the ordinary, I just happened to be there when you needed someone to talk to.”

12
Qaabeel said: “You are a good friend and good company.”

13
Iblees grinned.

14
Qaabeel armed himself and all the ablebodied members of his family and headed for Mecca.

15
In Mecca Qaabeel met Hibatullah and said: "I am your eldest brother Qaabeel, and as the firstborn I have come to claim my right to the Caliphate, the Divine Book, my father's beard hairs and the white silkspread with the printed faces."

16
Hibatullah said: "You have no place here. Go back whence you came."

17
Qaabeel said: "The Sacred Land of Mecca is my home."

18
Hibatullah said: "That was in the past."

19
Qaabeel said: "The past or the present, it is all the same to me. I have come to stay."

20
Hibatullah said: "My father banished you from the Sacred Land of Mecca."

21
Qaabeel said: "My father banished me in a fit of anger."

22
Hibatullah said: "I promised my father to keep you out of the Sacred Land of Mecca."

23
Qaabeel said: "No matter what you do you cannot erase the memory of me being born and brought up in the Sacred Land of Mecca."

24
Hibatullah said: "You are not wanted here. Every speck of life in the Sacred Land of Mecca has not forgotten you killed Haabeel."

25
Qaabeel said: "I had to kill Haabeel because Allah accepted his offering instead of mine, and I didnt want Haabeel to have children to boast over my children 'We are the children of Haabeel whose offering was accepted by Allah, and you are the children of Qaabeel whose offering was rejected by Allah'. I am the firstborn, and as the firstborn I am the rightful heir."

26
Hibatullah said: "You forfeited your right as the firstborn when you killed Haabeel."

27
Qaabeel said: "Haabeel tried to deprive me of what Allah had given me. I had to act to defend what was rightfully mine."

28
Hibatullah said: "It was Allah's Will that Haabeel should have what you claim to be yours."

29
Qaabeel said: "The rightful claim of the firstborn was Allah's idea, not mine."

30
Hibatullah said: “But Allah changed His Mind before you killed Haabeel.”

31
Qaabeel said: “Allah cannot change His Mind at will.”

32
Hibatullah said: “As Allah is our Creator and Provider He can do what He likes with us. We have to obey Him.”

33
Qaabeel said: “You can say whatever you like, but that doesnt alter the fact that I am the firstborn and the rightful heir. I warn you, if you dont acknowledge me as Allah’s Caliph and give me the Divine Book, my father’s beard hairs and the white silkspread with the printed faces I will kill you as I killed Haabeel.”

34
Hibatullah said: “My father had disinherited you and cursed you out of the Sacred Land of Mecca. If you dont leave peacefully I will forcibly throw you and your children out of the Sacred Land of Mecca.”

35
Qaabeel consulted Iblees: “What do you say to Hibatullah’s threat?”

36
Iblees said: “War.”

37
Qaabeel said: “War it will be.”

38
War flared up between the children of Adam and Hawwa.

39
Iblees and his soldier Shayaateen joined forces with Qaabeel.

40
Hibatullah saw Iblees and his soldier Shayaateen and drew the Divine Book out of its box and raised it heavenwards and called for Allah’s help: “Lord, help us defeat your enemies.”

41
Allah dispatched his soldier angels to help Hibatullah.

42
Iblees saw Allah’s soldier angels and said to his soldier Shayaateen: “Hold your weapons. Now that we have worked up the children of Adam and Hawwa and Allah’s soldier angels, let us watch them kill themselves.”

43
Qaabeel, outnumbered and outsworded, was defeated.

44
Qaabeel said to Hibatullah: “I am your eldest brother and your prisoner. If you kill me Allah will not forgive you.”

45
Hibatullah said: "You never gave Haabeel a chance, and my father wanted you dead. I will hand you over to the angels, and it will be up to them to decide what to do with you."

46
Qaabeel said to Iblees: "It is the end, my friend. Look after my children and ensure the Fire of Allah never stops burning."

47
Iblees said: "I will do all I can for your children, and rest assured, my friend, the Fire of Allah will never stop burning."

48
Hibatullah freed Qaabeel's children and said: "Go back to your homeland and never come anywhere near the Sacred Land of Mecca."

49
Qaabeel's children were happy to be free and back in Aden worshipping the Fire of Allah.

50
Hibatullah handed Qaabeel over to the angels, and the angels chained Qaabeel and whisked him to the eye of the sun in the west and left him facing the sun until his life was sunned out of him.

51
The angels delivered Qaabeel's body to Qaabeel's eldest son Shawhal and taught him the burial rites.

52
Shawhal and his twin sister Nawha were the handsomest of the children of Adam and Hawwa.

53
As the children of Qaabeel were about to bury their father, Iblees said to them: "No need to bury your father. This way you will lose him for good. Do you want to lose your father for good?"

54
Shawhal said to Iblees: "Of course not, but the angels told us to bury him."

55
Iblees said to Shawhal: "And you trust the word of the killers of your father?"

56
Shawhal said: "They said they were the angels of Allah and it was Allah's Will we bury our father."

57
Iblees said: "Shawhal, if Allah had wanted your father to be buried He would have conveyed His Will through His Fire in the temple, and not through the killers of your father."

58
Shawhal said: "What should we do?"

59
Iblees said: "Leave it to me and I will bring back your father."

60
Shawhal said: "How will you do that?"

61
Iblees said: "Shawhal, there is nothing I cannot do. I will sculpt a statue resembling your father and put your father's body inside the statue, and your father will become a living statue. You can keep the living statue of your father in your home or, better still, keep him in the temple of the Fire of Allah so he can be close to Allah. In the temple you can all visit the living statue of your father and talk to him about whatever you like. And if you want anything from Allah, just tell the living statue of your father about it and he will make sure Allah grants you your wish."

62
Shawhal said: "Do whatever you think is right."

63
Iblees sculpted a twopiece hollow statue out of a crystal block and embalmed Qaabeel's body with antishrivel ointments and dressed it with fine clothes and put it inside the hollow statue, then seated the stuffed statue on a gold chair.

64
The living statue looked the image of Qaabeel.

65
Iblees placed the living statue of Qaabeel in the temple of the Fire of Allah, and appointed Shawhal as its high priest and Qaabeel's successor, and gave him the title of Mukarrib to stress his closeness to Allah through the living statue of his father.

66
Iblees said to Qaabeel's children: "As your eldest brother Shawhal is your Mukarrib and high priest, you will need his permission to visit the living statue of your father. And when you visit the living statue of your father bow to him three times and kiss his hand."

67
Shawhal swelled with pride and said to Iblees: "You are to me as you were to my father."

68
Iblees said to Qaabeel's children: "My friends, now that your father is alive again, let us celebrate the day the angels killed your father as an Eid, a feastday of music, song, dance, drink and pleasure thrills, so that the Eid will always remind your father's killers of their failure in blotting out your father and the memory of your father."

69
Iblees entrusted one of his soldier Shayaateen to guard the living statue of Qaabeel and to listen to what the visitors say to it and report everything to him.

70
Every time the living statue was visited, Iblees appeared to the visitors in their dreams and told them their wishes would come true on waking.

71
Once in a while Iblees slipped into the living statue of Qaabeel and talked to the visitors through its mouth, and the visitors thought they were talking to their father.

72
As the years rolled on the living statue of Qaabeel was worshipped as a father god who loved and protected his children and made sure Allah granted their wishes.

GLOSSARY

Abqar:	the wadi of the genius, retreat of Iblees in Hadramawt (Yemen).
Adam:	to mix, brown, colour of soil, from earth.
Adan:	home, to settle down, home paradise of Adam and Hawwa, third paradise.
Adeem:	brown, soil, first earth.
Afyah:	wide, scented, wadi in Jannat Adan.
Akhbar:	history, historical narratives.
Akhbar poem:	historical narrative poem.
Allah:	the refuge and beyond vision worshipped God of love on high, contraction of the article "al" and "ilah" (god on high).
Bab Tawba:	gate of atonement.
Basheer:	harbinger of good news, judge angel of miniparadise grave.
Buraaq:	winged riding creature with a human face.
Caliph:	successor, representative, offspring.
Dar Hayaat:	house of immortality.
Genie:	invisible, from Janna, Jahili deity.
Haabeel:	gift of Allah, second son of Adam killed by his elder brother Qaabeel, major Jahili god worshipped as Hubal.
Haarith:	the firepoker ploughman merchant, first name of Iblees.
Hajj:	pilgrimage, annual.
Hamilard:	carrier of the earth, angel carrying the seven earths.

Hamilsama: carrier of heaven, angel carrying the seven heavens.

Hayaat: life, river of immortality.

Hayya: alive, serpent, the serpent that helped Iblees get into paradise.

Hazqyaa'eel: discipline of Allah.

Houri: paradisial, beautiful blackeyed girl.

Iblees: hopelessness, despair and gloom, Jahili god.

Israafeel: unlimited bounty and power of Allah.

Jabal: mountain.

Jabal Raahoon mountain in Sri Lanka known as Adam's Peak.

Jahannam: a very deep pit, first hell.

Janna: a garden of palm and vine trees, home garden, paradise.

Jannat Adan: metropolis of the seven paradises, third paradise.

Jannat Firdaws: paradise of vineyards, gardens and fertile wadis, sixth paradise.

Jannat Jalaal: paradise of majestic splendour, first paradise.

Jannat Khuld: paradise of immortality, fifth paradise.

Jannat Ma'wa: paradise of eternal refuge, fourth paradise.

Jannat Na'eem: paradise of eternal joy, seventh paradise.

Jannat Salaam: paradise of eternal peace, second paradise.

Jareer: on leash, pet lamb of Haabeel.

Jibreel: the power and blessing of Allah, angel of war and winds and earthquakes.

Ka'ba:	a squareshaped structure built by Adam in Mecca which has survived to this day as the Muslims' holiest shrine and centre of pilgrimage.
Karoobi:	close to Allah, angels of the sixth paradise.
Kawthar:	abundance, river of abundance in the sixth paradise.
Khuld Tree:	tree of immortality in the fifth paradise.
Labbaik:	at your (Allah's) will.
Lawh:	writing board, tablet.
Maalik:	proprietor, incharge, king, master, angel of the seven hells.
Ma'een:	flowing river in the fifth paradise.
Mikaa'eel:	the power and spring water of Allah, angel of rain and vegetation.
Mina:	wish, mountain near Mecca.
Mubashshir:	harbinger of good news, judge angel of the miniparadise grave.
Mukarrib:	close to Allah, king and high priest, title of the ancient kings of Yemen, equivalent to the title of Imam.
Munkar:	rejected, denied, judge angel of the minihell grave.
Naar:	fire, hell, angel of fire.
Najm:	star.
Naseem:	breeze, angel of breeze.
Qasida:	poem, long poem.

Raheeq: nectar, river of nectar in the fifth paradise.

Ridwaan: pleased and satisfied, angel of the seven paradises.

Rooh: soul.

Salaam: greetings, peace.

Shaitaan (pl. Shayaateen): to move away, distant, serpent, Jahili deity.

Shaitaan's head: tree, serpent with an ugly crested head.

Sidrat Muntaha Tree: the end-of-limit lote tree in the seventh heaven.

Stone of Consolation: whiter-than-milk stone Adam brought with him from paradise and used to wipe his tears before putting it in the Ka'ba, but over the centuries the stone became black on account of being touched by sinners.

Sura: narrative form based on episodes and sequences, sign of glory, Qur'an chapter.

Talbiya: prayer that begins with the "Labbaik" formula.

Ta'oos: peacock, the peacock that helped Iblees get into paradise.

Tawaaf: circumambulation.

Tooba Tree: scented tree in the fifth paradise.

Walad Mukhallad (pl. Wuldaan Mukhalladoon): paradisial, immortal handsome young man.

Zabaaniya: police, police angels who help Maalik to run the seven hells.

Zanjabeel: ginger, river of ginger wine in the third paradise.

Zaqqoom Tree: the gripping tree of the swallowed fruit in the fifth hell whose fruit is the food of the infernals.

Zill Mamdood Tree: the tree of the extended shadow in the second paradise.